THE BEST OF

Simply COLORADO™

COOKBOOK

Colorado
Dietetic
Association

WESTCLIFFE

D1294470

westcliffepublishers.com

The Best of Simply Colorado™

International Standard Book Numbers
ISBN-10: 1-56579-575-X
ISBN-13: 978-1-56579-575-4

Editor: Shelley McGhee and Liz Silbaugh
Designer: Margaret McCullough (CPG) www.corvuspublishinggroup.com
Production Manager: Craig Keyzer

Published by:
Westcliffe Publishers, Inc.
P. O. Box 1261
Englewood, CO 80150

Printed in China by C & C Offset Printing Co., Ltd.

Library of Congress Cataloging-in-Publication Data

Colorado Dietetic Association.
  The best of simply Colorado cookbook / The Colorado Dietetic Association.
    p. cm.
  Includes index.
  ISBN-13: 978-1-56579-575-4
  ISBN-10: 1-56579-575-X
  1. Cookery, American. I. Title.
  TX715.C722933 2006
  641.5'973--dc22
                          2006022098

For more information about other fine books and calendars from Westcliffe Publishers, please contact your
local bookstore, call us at 1-800-523-3692, or visit us on the web at **westcliffepublishers.com**.

The author and publisher of this book have made every effort to ensure the accuracy and
currency of its information. Nevertheless, books can require revisions. Please feel free to let
us know if you find information in this book that needs to be updated, and we will be glad to
correct it for the next printing. Your comments and suggestions are always welcome.

Acknowledgements

Compiling a cookbook is a monumental task, requiring the coordination, organization, and devotion of many individuals.

The Colorado Dietetic Association would like to acknowledge the following persons for their time and efforts to the *Simply Colorado*™ cookbook series:

Kay Petre Massey, R. D., Editor and Cookbook Committee/Steering Committee Chairman for both *Simply Colorado*: *Nutritious Recipes for Busy People* and *Simply Colorado,*™ *Too!: More Nutritious Recipes for Busy People*; Mary Lee Chin, M. S., R. D.; Liz Marr, M. S., R. D.; and Stephanie Smith, M. S., R. D., for their assistance in publicity and marketing; Tami Anderson, R. D., President, Simply Colorado, Inc. Board of Directors; Shelley McGhee, M. S., R. D., for chairing *The Best of Simply Colorado*™ edition; Laura Brieser-Smith, M. P. H., R. D.; Heidi Fritz, R. D.; Erica Gradwell, M. S., R. D.; and Pat Stiles, M. S., R. D., for retesting and re-evaluating the many recipes compiled for this cookbook; Randy Erickson, Executive Director of Simply Colorado, Inc., for more than ten years of accounting, order filling, storing, shipping, tracking, advertising, and selling the *Simply Colorado*™ cookbooks.

The Best of Simply Colorado™

Table of Contents

Introduction

In the late 1980s, members of the Colorado Dietetic Association embarked on a fantastic journey into the world of cookbook publishing. The result and final destination: *Simply Colorado: Nutritious Recipes for Busy People*, published in 1989. The overwhelming success of *Simply Colorado* led to a second book called *Simply Colorado, Too!: More Nutritious Recipes for Busy People*, released in 1999. Sales of these books soared above the 150,000 mark. *Simply Colorado* led with more than 125,000 copies sold—a milestone for any cookbook.

To celebrate our success, we present to you our newest addition to the Simply Colorado family, *The Best of Simply Colorado*. In this cookbook we combine favorite recipes from both cookbooks. Reflecting changes in dietary guidelines, eating habits, and food choices, *The Best of Simply Colorado* offers the quick and easy, tasty and healthy recipes you expect from Colorado's food and nutrition experts (registered dietitians).

Also, recognizing that Colorado continues to be a cultural crossroads, *The Best of Simply Colorado* includes an assortment of recipes from the desert Southwest to the fragrant and flavorful Orient.

The Best of Simply Colorado also provides:

- Complete nutrition analyses with each recipe to include calories, proteins, carbohydrates, fat, saturated fat, cholesterol, fiber, and sodium.
- More mouthwatering entrées in our Vegetarian section than in either of the previous editions.
- An updated look that makes *The Best of Simply Colorado* an appealing book to page through, use, and place in your cookbook collection.

As you ponder these changes, take a few moments to sit back, relax, and explore *The Best of Simply Colorado*. We think you'll like what you see and what we have to offer.

History 101

The idea for the *Simply Colorado*™ cookbooks came about for many reasons. Chiefly, registered dietitians noticed that their clients wanted to maintain and achieve good health. However, many of them didn't know how to prepare meals that were both lower in calories and tasty to eat. Many clients also wanted simple recipes, with few ingredients, to fit in with a fast-paced lifestyle.

Responding to this need, the Colorado Dietetic Association asked its members to submit and test recipes that met the following criteria: The recipes had to be flavorful, quick to prepare, and use fewer ingredients than more traditional recipes. They also had to be low in calories and fat and have more essential nutrients than their traditional counterparts.

The first two *Simply Colorado*™ cookbooks emanated from the hundreds of recipes collected and triple-tested by registered dietitians throughout Colorado.

All of the recipes in this cookbook were analyzed for their nutritional composition using the *ESHA Food Processor*® software program. Values for total calories, proteins, carbohydrates, fat, saturated fat, cholesterol, fiber, and sodium are at the end of each recipe.

Please note:

+   The nutritional information represents the lowest values, when you make the recipe with the lowest fat-containing ingredient(s). For example, if a recipe can be made with either nonfat or lowfat yogurt, the nutritional values printed after the recipe reflect those for the nonfat yogurt variation.

+   Though these recipes represent healthy cuisine, they are not intended for specific dietary restrictions, and should not replace the advice of a physician or a registered dietitian.

Just the Facts, Please

Food trends and fads of the latter part of the twentieth century swayed between choosing high-fat, no-fat, no-carbohydrate, and high-carbohydrate diets, all to the detriment of health and welfare.

In the interest of lowering fat and calories, many have forgotten the larger picture: Namely, that achieving good health, through good nutrition, means choosing a variety of whole foods, such as whole grains, beans, fresh fruits, vegetables, dairy products, and lean meats.

Relying on nonfat and fat-free food products, and stocking the pantry full of these items, is not the way toward better nutritional status. In fact, some fats are essential—meaning that they must come from the food we eat, because our bodies cannot make them.

If there is one myth to dispel from all the diet fads and trends it is this fact: It is the total calories we eat, coupled with the amount of exercise we get, that determines weight gain or loss.

If we eat more calories than we burn through exercise, we will gain weight. Conversely, if we use up more calories than we bring in, we will lose weight. The equation sounds simple, but most of us know that maintaining a healthy weight is a difficult task. There are many factors that affect how our bodies process the foods we eat.

It is not within the scope of this cookbook to discuss in great detail the ways to achieve good health. However, there are some recommendations, courtesy of the United States government, that we can take to heart and follow. They are called the U. S. Dietary Guidelines, and they are re-evaluated and updated every five years.

U. S. Dietary Guidelines: 2005

The goal of the dietary guidelines is to promote health and prevent disease. Here, the guidelines remind us to:

- Consume a variety of nutrient-rich foods and beverages from the basic food groups (see My Pyramid). Focus on choosing nutrient-rich foods first because these foods provide a substantial amount of nutrients per calorie level. This recommendation is especially critical at a time when many Americans are consuming too many calories but still falling short on nutrients.

- Try lean meats, beef, pork, game, and poultry to reduce saturated fat intake; broaden the sources of protein to include mixtures of beans (legumes), whole grains, tofu, nuts, and nut butters, because these proteins are cholesterol-free and are higher in heart-healthy polyunsaturated fats. Likewise, choose fat-free or low-fat dairy products. Use whole milk products sparingly.

- Be physically active to prevent chronic diseases, weight gain, and osteoporosis. Exercise at least thirty minutes a day. If you're just beginning an exercise program, set small, achievable goals. Walking for ten minutes, three times daily is as beneficial as walking thirty minutes non-stop.

- Aim for 20 to 30 percent of total calories from fat, mostly from polyunsaturated and monounsaturated sources, such as fish, nuts, and vegetable oils. Keep saturated fats to less than 10 percent of total calories, and limit cholesterol to 300 mgs per day, to reduce risk of heart disease. Keep trans-fat (chemically altered or hydrogenated fat) intake as low as possible.

- Eat potassium-rich foods, because potassium regulates blood pressure and prevents hypertension. Generally, all foods have potassium, but they have more of this mineral when they're in their whole, natural form. Good sources of potassium are bananas, citrus fruit, cantaloupe, mangos, tomatoes, potatoes, beans, whole grains, and dairy products.

- Limit processed foods, because processed foods replace potassium with sodium (salt), and have more calories and refined sugar than whole foods, or foods made from scratch. For good health, we should aim for less than one teaspoon (2,300 mgs) of salt daily.

- Drink alcoholic beverages in moderation: One drink daily for women; two drinks daily for men.

The Colorado Dietetic Association supports the U. S. Dietary Guidelines and encourages everyone to use the MyPyramid to plan diets that help maintain healthy weight, reduce the risk of disease, and achieve good nutritional status.

The Power of the Pyramid

MyPyramid presents each food group, using colored stripes. The stripes on the pyramid are thick or thin, depending on the number of daily servings.

Here are some examples of how much food to consume each day from each of the MyPyramid food groups. This example is based on consuming 2,000 calories a day. (Visit the website www.mypyramid.gov to get your own personalized pyramid.)

MyPyramid
A Guide to Daily Food Choices

Grains
Eat 6 ounces every day; make half your grains whole

Vegetables
Eat 2 ½ cups every day

Milk
Get 3 cups every day

Fruit
Eat 2 cups every day

Meat and Beans
Eat 5 ½ ounces every day

MyPyramid
STEPS TO A HEALTHIER YOU
MyPyramid.gov

GRAINS   VEGETABLES   FRUITS   MILK   MEAT & BEANS

Internal Temperatures for Food Safety

To be sure that cooked meats, poultry, and egg dishes are safe, it is best to test internal temperatures with a food thermometer. Not all of the recipes in the book include the recommended internal temperatures. Use the chart below as a reference to determine safe internal temperatures of cooked food.

Product Temperature °F

Egg Dishes	160
Ground Meat and Meat Mixtures	160
Fresh Beef, Veal, Lamb	
Medium Rare	145
Medium	160
Well Done	170
Pork (all cuts including ground)	
Medium	160
Well Done	170
Poultry	
Whole Chicken or Turkey	180
Stuffing (cooked separately)	165
Chicken Breast	165
Chicken Thigh	180
Ham	
Fresh (cooked from raw)	160
Fully cooked (to reheat)	140

Modifying Your Favorite Recipes

Eating healthy doesn't mean giving up all of your favorite recipes. By modifying your recipes to include lower-calorie ingredients and lower-calorie cooking methods, many will easily fit into a healthy diet. To get started, ask these questions about your recipe:

- Do any of the ingredients come in a low-calorie, or low-sodium version?
- Are all the ingredients essential?
- Can the recipe be cooked by a method that requires less fat, or a healthier fat, and calories?

In modifying recipes, there a few things to remember:

- The goal is to decrease calories without sacrificing taste and texture.
- When you reduce the amount of fat in a recipe, you may need to replace it with something that enhances the flavor of the recipe: other liquids, sugar, sugar-free flavors, and herbs and spices are examples of flavor enhancers.
- Liquid oils can be reduced and/or replaced with other liquids, such as water, milk, wine, fruit juice, or broth.
- Butter and margarine can be replaced with liquid oils in some recipes: 16 tablespoons equals 1 cup. Three teaspoons equals 1 tablespoon.

For a quick lesson in modifying recipes for healthier results, compare the following original and light versions of Garlic Shrimp on a Bun. Then, take what you've learned and apply it to some of your own favorite recipes. Don't be afraid to experiment; you'll be surprised just how often experiments turn into new favorites.

Garlic Shrimp on a Bun

1/2 c. green onion *OK*
2–3 cloves garlic, minced *OK*
~~1 c. butter, melted~~ *2 tsp. olive oil*
~~1 T.~~ white wine *increase to 2/3 cup (to improve flavor)*
~~1 tsp.~~ lemon juice *increase to 1/4 cup (to improve flavor)*
1/8 tsp. salt *OK*
1/8 tsp. pepper *OK*
1 tsp. dried dillweed *OK*
1 1/2 lbs. large fresh shrimp, peeled and de-veined *OK*
2 French rolls, split lengthwise, ~~brushed with butter~~ and toasted

Substitutions

When Your Recipe Calls For:	Try This:
Meat and Eggs	**Meat and Eggs**
1 whole egg	2 egg whites or 1/4 cup egg substitute
2 strips of bacon	1 ounce lean ham or Canadian bacon
Ground beef	Ground turkey
Expensive high-fat meats	Inexpensive lean meats
"Choice" and "Prime" cuts	"Select" cuts
Chicken with skin	Remove skin before cooking
Oil-packed tuna	Water-packed tuna
Dairy Products	**Dairy Products**
Whole milk	Skim, 1%, or 2% milk
Cream	Evaporated skim milk
Sour cream	Plain nonfat or lowfat yogurt, light sour cream, blended lowfat cottage cheese
Cream cheese	Light cream cheese (blended or lowfat) or dry curd cottage cheese
Cheddar cheese	Extra-sharp cheddar cheese, half amount
American, Cheddar, Colby, Monterey Jack, and Swiss cheeses	A cheese with 5 or fewer grams of fat cheeses per ounce (try "reduced-fat" varieties)
Mozzarella cheese	Part-skim mozzarella
Ricotta cheese	Light ricotta or part-skim
Ice cream	Lowfat, fat-free, or frozen nonfat or lowfat yogurt

Substitutions

When Your Recipe Calls For:	Try This:
Whipped cream	Evaporated skim milk, chilled until almost frozen, then whipped
Fruit	**Fruit**
Jam, jelly, or preserves	Pure-fruit spreads or reduced-sugar varieties
Syrup-packed canned fruit	Fresh fruit or fruit packed in own juice or water-packed
Fats	**Fats**
1/2 cup shortening	1/3 cup vegetable oil
1 cup butter	Equal amount margarine or 2/3 cup vegetable oil
Mayonnaise	Fat-free or light mayonnaise, plain nonfat or lowfat yogurt
1 ounce Baking chocolate	3 tablespoons cocoa plus 1 tablespoon margarine
Fudge sauce	Chocolate syrup
Nuts	Use fresh, unsalted
Salad dressing	Oil and vinegar or fresh lemon juice, fruit juice with low-sodium soy sauce, fresh-squeezed lemon or lime juice with salt and pepper to taste, light or lowfat-dressing
Condensed cream soups	99% fat-free condensed cream soups
Grease a pan	Lightly coat pan with cooking spray

Appetizers, Snacks, & Beverages

COLD APPETIZERS & SNACKS

HOT APPETIZERS & SNACKS

BEVERAGES

Cajun-Style Garbanzo Nuts

This spicy snack also makes a good salad topper.

Yield:
4 servings

Serving Size:
⅓ cup

Preparation Time:
5 minutes

Cooking Time:
45–55 minutes

1 can (15 ½ oz.) garbanzo beans
1½–1 tsp. black pepper
1 tsp. garlic powder
¼–½ tsp. cayenne pepper
¼ tsp. dried oregano leaves
½ tsp. salt (optional)
Cooking spray

Preheat oven to 325°. Drain and rinse beans. In a medium bowl, combine beans and all spices, tossing to coat. Spread on a baking sheet that has been lightly coated with cooking spray. Bake for 45–55 minutes, or until browned and crisp. Stir as needed to brown evenly.

Nutrition Analysis Per Serving:

Calories 88

Protein 5g

Carbohydrate 14g

Fat 1g

(Saturated Fat <1g)

Cholesterol 0mg

Fiber 4g

Sodium 288mg

These spicy Cajun-Style Garbanzo Nuts are a nutrient-rich, low-calorie snack. While regular nuts are about 77 percent fat, Garbanzo Nuts are only 9 percent fat.

Chili Popcorn

Keep this easy-to-make popcorn on hand in an airtight container.

**6 c. lowfat, low-sodium
microwave-popped popcorn
1 T. margarine, melted
½ tsp. chili powder
⅛ tsp. salt
⅛ tsp. garlic powder**

While popcorn is popping, combine melted margarine, chili powder, salt, and garlic powder. Drizzle mixture over warm popcorn. Toss gently to coat.

Yield:
6 servings

Serving Size:
1 cup

Preparation Time:
2–5 minutes

**Nutrition Analysis
Per Serving:**

Calories 43

Protein 1g

Carbohydrate 4g

Fat 2g

(Saturated Fat <1g)

Cholesterol 0mg

Fiber 1g

Sodium 101mg

Crispy Pita Wedges for Dipping

Yield:
24 servings

Serving Size:
1 wedge

Preparation Time:
5 minutes

Cooking Time:
3 minutes

3 (6 ½-inch) whole-wheat pita bread loaves
Olive oil cooking spray

Cut each pita loaf into 8 wedges. Separate each wedge into 2 pieces and place on cookie sheet, in-side up. Spray each piece with the olive oil cooking spray. Broil until crisp (about 3 minutes), being careful not to overcook. Serve with a favorite dip or two from the following pages.

Nutrition Analysis Per Serving:

Calories 22

Protein 1g

Carbohydrate 4g

Fat <1g

(Saturated Fat <1g)

Cholesterol 0mg

Fiber 1g

Sodium 56mg

Curry Yogurt Dip

This favorite dip adds an exotic flavor of India to your menu.

1 c. plain nonfat or lowfat yogurt
3 T. light mayonnaise
2 tsp. curry powder
¼ tsp. onion salt

Mix all ingredients together and chill. Serve as a dip with assorted vegetables or as a sauce with fish or chicken.

Yield:
10 servings

Serving Size:
2 tablespoons

Preparation Time:
5 minutes

Chilling Time:
20 minutes

Curry is a blend of many different spices, and there are many different curry mixes available in most supermarkets. Curries come in a dry, powdery mix, or bottled as a paste or sauce. When you're looking for a paste, buy the hottest available. You'll find that just a little bit goes a long way in flavoring any vegetable dish or main entrée. You'll use less, and the paste will last longer than a milder blend.

Nutrition Analysis Per Serving:

Calories 26

Protein 1g

Carbohydrate 3

Fat 2g

(Saturated Fat <1g)

Cholesterol 2mg

Fiber <1g

Sodium 96mg

Dilly Yogurt Dip

The delicate flavor of this dip is ideal when served with crudités for a picnic in the park or in the mountains. It's also a nice accompaniment with salmon or other fish.

Yield:
10 servings

Serving Size:
2 tablespoons

Preparation Time:
5 minutes

Chilling Time:
20 minutes

1 c. plain nonfat or lowfat yogurt
3 T. light mayonnaise
2 T. chopped green onions
½ tsp. dried dillweed
¼ tsp. onion salt
2 tsp. lemon juice
½ tsp. Dijon mustard
Pinch of sugar

Mix all ingredients together and chill for 20 minutes to let flavors blend. Serve as a dip with assorted vegetables or chips.

Nutrition Analysis Per Serving:

Calories 26

Protein 1g

Carbohydrate 3g

Fat 2g

(Saturated Fat 0g)

Cholesterol 2mg

Fiber <1g

Sodium 72mg

Substituting plain nonfat yogurt for sour cream creates a savings of 300 calories and 40 grams of fat in just one cup.

Spinach Dip with Bread Bowl

A simple and delicious dip with an elegant presentation.

1 pkg. (10 oz.) frozen, chopped spinach, thawed and well drained
1 c. plain nonfat or lowfat yogurt
⅓ c. light mayonnaise
1 pkg. dry onion soup mix
Hot pepper sauce, to taste
1 tsp. lemon juice
¼ tsp. black pepper
1 round rye loaf

Drain spinach and pat out excess moisture between two paper towels. Combine spinach with yogurt, mayonnaise, onion soup mix, hot pepper sauce, lemon juice, and pepper. Chill. Prepare bread by cutting a bowl from the center of the loaf. Cut removed bread into 1-inch cubes. Fill bread bowl with dip and serve with rye bread cubes and vegetables.

Using light mayonnaise is a great way to reduce fat and calories in your favorite recipes. Every tablespoon of light mayonnaise will save 60 calories and 7.5 grams of fat, compared to regular mayonnaise.

Yield:
24 servings

Serving Size:
2 tablespoons

Preparation Time:
10 minutes

Chilling Time:
30 minutes

Nutrition Analysis Per Serving:

Calories 41

Protein 2g

Carbohydrate 6g

Fat 1g

(Saturated Fat <1g)

Cholesterol 1mg

Fiber 1g

Sodium 139mg

Five-Minute Pesto Dip

Adults need 1,000 to 1,200 milligrams of calcium daily. This recipe gives you a good start toward reaching that amount.

Yield:
12 servings

Serving Size:
2 tablespoons

Preparation Time:
5 minutes

Chilling Time:
30 minutes

1 c. hot water
⅓ c. chopped sun-dried tomatoes
1 c. plain nonfat yogurt
¼ c. your favorite pesto sauce

Pour water over the sun-dried tomatoes in a bowl to hydrate. Let stand for 5 minutes, drain. Combine the sun-dried tomatoes, yogurt, and pesto sauce in a bowl and mix well. Cover and chill. Serve with fresh vegetables or *Crispy Pita Wedges* (p. 4).

Nutrition Analysis Per Serving:

Calories 42

Protein 2g

Carbohydrate 4g

Fat 3g

(Saturated Fat 1g)

Cholesterol 2mg

Fiber <1g

Sodium 109mg

Southwestern Layered Dip

A wonderfully easy appetizer to take to your next Broncos party!

1 can (15 oz.) black beans, drained and rinsed
1 can (4 oz.) chopped black olives, drained
1 small onion, finely chopped
2 T. fresh lime juice
1 T. olive oil
1 clove garlic, minced
¼ tsp. crushed red pepper
¼ tsp. cumin
¼ tsp. salt
⅛ tsp. black pepper
1 tub (8 oz.) light cream cheese
⅔ c. chopped tomato
⅓ c. chopped green onions

Combine the black beans, black olives, onion, lime juice, olive oil, garlic, red pepper, cumin, salt, and black pepper in a bowl and mix well. Chill, covered, for 2 hours or longer. Spread the cream cheese evenly on a 10-inch round serving plate. Spread the bean mixture over the cream cheese. Arrange the tomato in a ring around the outer edge. Sprinkle with the green onions. Serve with baked tortilla chips or *Salsa Fresca* (p. 10).

Traditional tortilla chips contain 6 grams of fat per serving while baked tortilla chips have only 1 gram of fat per serving.

Yield:
10 servings

Serving Size:
⅓ cup

Preparation Time:
15 minutes

Chilling Time:
2 hours

Nutrition Analysis Per Serving:

Calories 115

Protein 5g

Carbohydrate 10g

Fat 7g

(Saturated Fat 3g)

Cholesterol 11mg

Fiber 3g

Sodium 396mg

Salsa Fresca

Yield:
6 servings

Serving Size:
½ cup

Preparation Time:
20 minutes

Chilling Time:
30 minutes

3 c. diced tomatoes
1 jalapeño pepper, seeded and diced
1 can (4 oz.) chopped green chiles
½ c. chopped green onions
¼ c. chopped fresh cilantro
2–3 T. fresh lime juice
1 tsp. chili powder
1 tsp. dried oregano leaves
1 tsp. garlic salt

Combine all ingredients in a large mixing bowl. Refrigerate 30 minutes to allow flavors to blend.

Nutrition Analysis Per Serving:

Calories 27

Protein 1g

Carbohydrate 6g

Fat <1g

(Saturated Fat <1g)

Cholesterol 0mg

Fiber 2g

Sodium 240mg

Fresh cilantro can be found in the produce section of most supermarkets, it may be labeled as Chinese parsley. Cilantro doesn't hold up well under long periods of high heat, so add it toward the end of cooking to gain the best flavor.

Cripple Creek Caviar

Eating black-eyed peas is supposed to bring good luck. We know you'll hit the mother lode if you eat some before heading to the gambling town that gives this dish its name.

1 can (16 oz.) black-eyed peas, drained and rinsed
⅓ c. lowfat Italian dressing
1 can (4 oz.) chopped green chiles
1 T. vinegar
¼ tsp. Italian seasoning
Dash crushed red pepper flakes
2 tomatoes, chopped
¼ c. chopped green onion

Combine first 6 ingredients; cover and chill 4–6 hours. Add tomato and green onion; toss gently. Serve with cracker, *Crispy Pita Wedges* (p. 4), or Melba rounds.

High in soluble fiber (the kind that helps lower blood cholesterol), legumes are also a rich source of vegetable protein.

Yield:
10 servings

Serving Size:
¼ cup

Preparation Time:
10 minutes

Chilling Time:
4–6 hours

Nutrition Analysis Per Serving:

Calories 62

Protein 2g

Carbohydrate 9g

Fat 2g

(Saturated Fat <1g)

Cholesterol 0mg

Fiber 2g

Sodium 245mg

Colorado Crab Spread

Double the recipe and serve this delicious appetizer as a light supper.

Yield:
6 servings

Serving Size:
½ cup

Preparation Time:
15 minutes

1 lb. imitation crabmeat
2 T. lemon juice
2 T. plain nonfat or lowfat yogurt
¼ c. light mayonnaise
½ tsp. dried dillweed
¼ tsp. celery salt
½ c. finely chopped bell pepper
¼ c. finely chopped red onion
½ tsp. garlic powder

Cut crab into small pieces and toss with lemon juice in a medium-sized bowl. Add remaining ingredients and mix well. Serve with lowfat crackers.

Nutrition Analysis Per Serving:

Calories 130

Protein 11g

Carbohydrate 13g

Fat 4g

(Saturated Fat 1g)

Cholesterol 41mg

Fiber <1g

Sodium 171mg

Imitation crabmeat, or surimi, is made from mild-flavored fish such as pollock or cod, to which crab flavoring is added. This gives the product a distinctive crab taste without the high price.

Smoked Salmon Paté

Fancy enough for a special occasion—easy enough for anytime!

¼ c. chopped pecans
1 can (14 oz.) salmon, drained
1 tub (8 oz.) light cream cheese
2 T. grated onion
1 T. lemon juice
1 tsp. prepared horseradish
¼ tsp. salt
¼ tsp. liquid smoke
¼ c. finely chopped fresh parsley

Spread the pecans in a single layer on a baking sheet. Toast at 350° for 5 minutes or until light brown and fragrant. Let stand until cool. Mash the salmon in a bowl. Add the cream cheese, onion, lemon juice, horseradish, salt, and liquid smoke; mix well. Chill, covered, for 15 minutes.

Shape the salmon mixture into a ball. Roll in the parsley. Sprinkle the pecans over the top of the ball and press lightly. Chill, wrapped in plastic wrap, until serving time. Serve with crackers.

Light cream cheese in a tub saves about 8 grams of fat, compared to light cream cheese packaged as a block. This savings occurs because manufacturers whip the cream cheese. Whipping adds air to the product, giving tub cream cheese a lighter texture and fewer calories than its packaged counterpart.

Yield:
12 servings

Serving Size:
2 tablespoons

Preparation Time:
10 minutes

Chilling Time:
30 minutes

Nutrition Analysis Per Serving:

Calories 108

Protein 9g

Carbohydrate 2g

Fat 6g

(Saturated Fat 3g)

Cholesterol 22mg

Fiber <1g

Sodium 300mg

Mediterranean Yogurt Cheese

A tasty substitute for cream cheese, sour cream, or mayonnaise.

Yield:
½ cup

Serving Size:
1 tablespoon

Preparation Time:
3 minutes

Draining time:
12–24 hours

Nutrition Analysis Per Serving:

Calories 16

Protein 2g

Carbohydrate 2g

Fat 0g

(Saturated Fat 0g)

Cholesterol 1mg

Fiber 0g

Sodium 24mg

1 container (8 oz.) plain nonfat or lowfat yogurt (For best results, choose yogurt without gelatin)

To make yogurt cheese, place yogurt in a colander lined with cheesecloth or a coffee filter. Place colander over a bowl and cover loosely with plastic wrap; chill 12–24 hours. Discard liquid.

Blend ½ cup yogurt cheese with 2 tablespoons reduced-sugar strawberry preserves for a delicious topping for bagels. Or add ½ teaspoon dried dill or Italian seasoning for a sandwich spread that's much more nutritious than mayonnaise.

Nutty Apricot Cheese Spread

This unusual combination of flavors melds together for an outstanding spread that's sure to get rave reviews!

1 tub (8 oz.) light cream cheese
½ c. reduced-sugar apricot preserves or spread
¼ c. chopped green onion
¼ c. coarsely chopped dry-roasted peanuts

Run a knife around the outer edge of cream cheese to loosen; invert it onto a serving plate. Spread apricot preserves over cream cheese; top with green onion and peanuts. Serve immediately or refrigerate up to 1 hour. Serve with Melba rounds or other crispy crackers.

Yield:
8 servings

Serving Size:
2 tablespoons

Preparation Time:
5 minutes

Nutrition Analysis Per Serving:

Calories 118

Protein 4g

Carbohydrate 9g

Fat 7g

(Saturated Fat 3g)

Cholesterol 16mg

Fiber <1g

Sodium 85mg

Cool Garden Pizza

This make-ahead pizza is fun to take along for a picnic or concert at Red Rocks Park.

Yield:
12 servings

Serving Size:
2 pieces

Preparation Time:
30–35 minutes

Cooking Time:
15–20 minutes

Chilling Time:
20 minutes

Nutrition Analysis Per Serving:

Calories 193

Protein 9g

Carbohydrate 27g

Fat 7g

(Saturated Fat 2g)

Cholesterol 11mg

Fiber 4g

Sodium 310mg

1 loaf frozen whole-wheat bread dough
or prepared pizza crust, thawed
1 pkg. (8 oz.) light cream cheese, softened
1 pkg. Ranch salad dressing mix
1 ½ c. raw vegetables, finely grated
(cauliflower, broccoli, zucchini, celery)
½ c. chopped green onion
½ c. shredded carrot
½ c. finely chopped tomato, drained

Preheat oven to 350°. Stretch dough into a
15 ½ x 12-inch jellyroll pan and bake until
done (about 15–20 minutes); cool completely.
Blend cream cheese and Ranch dressing; mix
spread evenly on crust. Sprinkle vegetables,
green onion, carrots, and tomato over
cream cheese mixture. Press in gently; chill.
Cut into 24 bite-sized pieces and serve.

Fresh Tomato Antipasto

This authentic Italian recipe is impressive, and easy to make.

1 lb. ripe tomatoes, chopped
(about 3 medium)
2 cloves garlic, minced
2 T. finely chopped fresh basil leaves
⅛ c. chopped fresh parsley
1 T. olive oil
Salt and freshly ground black pepper, to taste

Yield:
8 servings

Serving Size:
¼ cup

Preparation Time:
7–10 minutes

Lightly salt tomatoes and let them drain in colander. Combine garlic, basil, and parsley; mix with olive oil. Season to taste with salt and pepper. Toss tomatoes and herb mixture set aside. Serve with *Crispy Pita Wedges* (p. 4).

Nutrition Analysis Per Serving:

Calories 27

Protein 1g

Carbohydrate 3g

Fat 2g

(Saturated Fat <1g)

Cholesterol 0mg

Fiber 1g

Sodium 4mg

Dried herbs taste stronger than fresh herbs because the flavor is more concentrated. A good rule of thumb for substitution is to use 1 teaspoon dried herbs for 1 tablespoon fresh.

Salmon-Stuffed Cherry Tomatoes

This elegant appetizer will add color and excitement to your party fare.

Yield:
18 servings

Serving Size:
1 tomato

Preparation Time:
15 minutes

Chilling Time:
20 minutes

18 cherry tomatoes
6 oz. smoked salmon
⅓ c. light cream cheese
½ tsp. Worcestershire sauce

Cut the tops off of each tomato. Scoop out pulp, leaving shells intact. Invert tomato shells on paper towels to drain. Combine salmon, cream cheese, and Worcestershire sauce; stir well. Spoon 1 ½ teaspoons of stuffing into each tomato. Chill and serve.

Nutrition Analysis Per Serving:

Calories 24

Protein 2g

Carbohydrate 1g

Fat 1g

(Saturated Fat 1g)

Cholesterol 5mg

Fiber <1g

Sodium 90mg

Cheese-Topped Cherry Tomatoes

18 cherry tomatoes
8 oz. 1% cottage cheese, drained
1 T. finely chopped green onions
½ tsp. caraway seed
¼ tsp. your favorite seasoned salt

Cut tops off of each tomato. Scoop out pulp, leaving shells intact. Invert tomato shells on paper towels to drain. Combine cottage cheese, onion, caraway seeds, and salt; stir well. Spoon 1 ½ teaspoons of stuffing into each tomato. Chill and serve.

Yield:
18 servings

Serving Size:
1 tomato

Preparation Time:
15 minutes

Chilling Time:
20 minutes

Nutrition Analysis Per Serving:

Calories 12

Protein 2g

Carbohydrate 1g

Fat <1g

(Saturated Fat <1g)

Cholesterol 1mg

Fiber <1g

Sodium 22mg

Herbed Deviled Eggs

You'll be delighted with this lower-cholesterol version of deviled eggs.

Yield:
12 servings

Serving Size:
1 stuffed egg half

Preparation Time:
10–15 minutes

Chilling Time:
1–2 hours

6 hard-cooked eggs
3 T. 1% cottage cheese, drained
2 T. plain nonfat or lowfat yogurt
1 T. finely chopped onion
1 tsp. Dijon mustard
¼ tsp. dried dillweed
⅛ tsp. garlic powder
Dash hot pepper sauce
Salt and black pepper to taste (optional)

Cut eggs in half. Put half of the yolks into a small bowl; reserve remaining yolks for another use or discard. With fork, mash yolks together with cottage cheese and yogurt. Stir in remaining ingredients. Fill egg halves and chill. If desired, garnish with dill before serving.

Nutrition Analysis Per Serving:

Calories 39

Protein 3g

Carbohydrate 1g

Fat 2g

(Saturated Fat 1g)

Cholesterol 93 mg

Fiber <1g

Sodium 53g

Recommendations to "lower fat and cholesterol" don't mean "never eat meat or eggs" because they contain cholesterol. It is the total amount of fat and cholesterol in your diet that matters. Balance high-fat food with other foods that contain less fat and cholesterol.

Sun-Dried Tomato Crostini

1 oz. sun-dried tomatoes
1 c. boiling water
¼ c. pitted Kalamata olives
1 T. capers
1 T. olive oil
2 cloves garlic, minced
1 French bread baguette,
cut into ½-inch slices
1 tub (8 oz.) light cream cheese, softened
2 T. fresh basil, cut in ribbons

Yield:
24 servings

Serving Size:
1 crostini

Preparation Time:
10 minutes

Cooking Time:
10 minutes

Pour boiling water over the sun-dried tomatoes in a heat-resistant bowl to hydrate. Let stand for 2 minutes; drain. Combine the sun-dried tomatoes, olives, capers, olive oil, and garlic in a blender or food processor and process until smooth.

Arrange the bread slices in a single layer on a baking sheet. Bake at 400° for 8–10 minutes or until golden brown. Spread the cream cheese on the bread slices. Top with the tomato mixture and sprinkle with the basil.

Tip: Assemble the crostini just before serving.

Sun-dried tomatoes make a flavorful addition to many recipes. Substitute re-hydrated sun-dried tomatoes for the oil-packed version to decrease calories. One-third cup oil-packed sun-dried tomatoes contains 24 grams of fat. An equal amount of re-hydrated sun-dried tomatoes contains only 1 gram of fat.

Nutrition Analysis Per Serving:

Calories 81

Protein 3g

Carbohydrate 11g

Fat 3g

(Saturated Fat 1g)

Cholesterol 4mg

Fiber 1g

Sodium 223mg

Caraway Jack Potato Skins

This sporty appetizer tastes even better than traditional deep-fried "skins."

Yield:
6 servings

Serving Size:
4 pieces

Preparation Time:
20–25 minutes

Cooking Time:
10–15 minutes

3 medium potatoes, baked
Cooking spray
½ c. (2 oz.) shredded reduced-fat Monterey Jack cheese
½ tsp. caraway seeds
½ tsp. chili powder
½ tsp. paprika
1 tsp. grated Parmesan cheese

Preheat oven to 450°. Cut each potato in quarters lengthwise, and then in half crosswise to form 8 sections. Scoop pulp from skins, leaving ⅛-inch in the shells. Reserve pulp for another use or discard. Lightly spray both sides of the skins with cooking spray. Place on baking sheet; bake 10–12 minutes until crisp. (Skins can be made ahead to this point and reheated before filling.) Fill skins with Monterey Jack cheese then sprinkle with caraway seeds, chili powder, paprika, and Parmesan cheese. Place under broiler; heat just until cheese is melted. Serve hot.

Nutrition Analysis Per Serving:

Calories 140

Protein 5g

Carbohydrate 26g

Fat 2g

(Saturated Fat 1g)

Cholesterol 5mg

Fiber 2g

Sodium 85mg

Potatoes are naturally rich in complex carbohydrates, potassium, and vitamin C. Eating potato skins gives you the added bonus of a healthy dose of fiber.

Oven-Fried Zucchini Sticks

Kids will love these sticks whether they're dipped in spaghetti sauce or served on their own.

¼ c. Italian breadcrumbs
1 T. grated Parmesan cheese
⅛ tsp. garlic powder
2 medium zucchini
1 tsp. olive oil
3 T. water
Cooking spray
1 c. your favorite lowfat spaghetti sauce

Preheat oven to 475°. Combine breadcrumbs, Parmesan cheese, and garlic powder in a shallow dish; set aside. Cut each zucchini lengthwise into 4 pieces; cut each piece in half crosswise. Place pieces in a zip-top plastic bag. Add oil and water; shake. Dredge zucchini in breadcrumb mixture and place on baking sheet coated with cooking spray. Bake for 10 minutes or until brown and tender. Serve with warm spaghetti sauce.

Eating five to nine daily servings of fruits and vegetables is important for good health. Eating a variety of fruits and vegetables gives you the vitamin C, vitamin A, and fiber your body needs.

Yield:
8 servings

Serving Size:
2 sticks

Preparation Time:
15 minutes

Cooking Time:
10 minutes

Nutrition Analysis Per Serving:

Calories 40

Protein 1g

Carbohydrate 5g

Fat 2g

(Saturated Fat <1g)

Cholesterol 1mg

Fiber <1g

Sodium 192mg

Savory Stuffed Mushrooms

Everyone will be reaching for this flavorful appetizer.

Yield:
8 servings

Serving Size:
2 mushrooms

Preparation Time:
25 minutes

Cooking Time:
15–20 minutes

16 large mushrooms
Cooking spray
¼ c. finely chopped green pepper
¼ c. finely chopped onion
1 ½ c. soft breadcrumbs (about 4 slices)
½ c. (2 oz.) reduced-fat Monterey Jack cheese, shredded
½ tsp. salt
½ tsp. dried whole thyme
¼ tsp. turmeric
¼ tsp. black pepper

Preheat oven to 350°. Clean mushrooms and remove stems. Finely chop ⅓ cup stems, reserving remaining stems for another use. Set mushroom caps aside. Sauté chopped stems, green pepper, and onion in a non-stick skillet coated with cooking spray until tender. Remove from heat; stir in remaining ingredients (except mushroom caps). Evenly spoon stuffing into reserved mushroom caps. Bake for 15–20 minutes.

Hint: Mushrooms may be stuffed ahead of time and kept in refrigerator until ready to bake.

Never wash mushrooms until you are ready to use them. To wash, simply wipe them with a damp paper towel.

Nutrition Analysis Per Serving:

Calories 56

Protein 4g

Carbohydrate 7g

Fat 2g

(Saturated Fat 1g)

Cholesterol 5mg

Fiber 1g

Sodium 265mg

Stuffed Mushrooms Florentine

An elegant appetizer for a special occasion.

1 pkg. (10 oz.) frozen chopped
spinach, thawed
1 c. herb-seasoned bread stuffing cubes
1 egg
1 T. margarine, melted
¼ c. grated Parmesan cheese
1 tsp. garlic salt
¼ tsp. dried thyme
Freshly ground black pepper to taste
20 fresh mushrooms

Preheat oven to 350°. Drain spinach and pat out excess moisture between two paper towels. Combine all ingredients except mushrooms; mix well. Clean mushrooms; remove stems and discard. Evenly spoon stuffing into each mushroom cap. Bake on an ungreased baking sheet for 15–20 minutes.

Store loose mushrooms in the refrigerator in a paper bag or open container loosely covered. Mushrooms stored in plastic bags deteriorate quickly, because the bags trap moisture.

Yield:
10 servings

Serving Size:
2 mushrooms

Preparation Time:
10 minutes

Cooking Time:
20 minutes

Nutrition Analysis Per Serving:

Calories 72

Protein 4g

Carbohydrate 7g

Fat 3g

(Saturated Fat 1g)

Cholesterol 23mg

Fiber 2g

Sodium 259mg

Teriyaki Ribbons

For a unique appetizer with a distinctive Asian flavor, add this to your menu.

Yield:
24 servings

Serving Size:
2 skewers

Preparation Time:
5–10 minutes

Marinating Time:
1 hour

Cooking Time:
8–10 minutes

1 ½ lbs. flank steak
¾ c. Teriyaki sauce
2 large cloves garlic, minced
1 tsp. ground ginger
1 tsp. crushed red pepper flakes

Cut steak diagonally, against the grain, into ¼-inch slices. (Slicing is easiest when beef has been put in the freezer for 1 hour and is partially frozen.) Combine Teriyaki and seasonings. Marinate steak for 1 hour in Teriyaki marinade. Lace steak slices on bamboo skewers. Broil or grill skewers on both sides until done.

Nutrition Analysis Per Serving:

Calories 62

Protein 6g

Carbohydrate 3g

Fat 3g

(Saturated Fat 1g)

Cholesterol 12mg

Fiber <1g

Sodium 220mg

To keep bamboo skewers from burning while the meat is cooking, soak them in water for 15 minutes before threading the meat.

Lemon-Strawberry Punch

8 oz. frozen lemonade concentrate, thawed
1 pkg. (10 oz.) frozen strawberries, thawed
1 quart ginger ale or lemon-lime soda
Ice

Mix lemonade and strawberries
together. Add ginger ale or lemon-lime
soda and ice just before serving.

Tip: To reduce calories, try using diet soda.

Yield:
20 servings

Serving Size:
½ cup

Preparation Time:
5–10 minutes

**Nutrition Analysis
Per Serving:**

Calories 42

Protein <1g

Carbohydrate 11g

Fat <1g

(Saturated Fat 0g)

Cholesterol 0mg

Fiber <1g

Sodium 4mg

Mock Sangria

Try this award-winning drink—it tastes better than the real thing!

Yield:
28 servings

Serving Size:
½ cup

Preparation Time:
5–10 minutes

1 bottle (40 oz.) unsweetened white grape juice, chilled
1 bottle (32 oz.) apple-cranberry juice, chilled
½ c. lime juice, chilled
1 bottle (33.8 oz.) club soda, chilled

Garnish:
Seedless green grapes
Sliced limes
Sliced oranges

Combine juices. Just before serving, add club soda; stir and garnish.

Nutrition Analysis Per Serving:

Calories 52

Protein <1g

Carbohydrate 13g

Fat <1g

(*Saturated Fat <1g*)

Cholesterol 0mg

Fiber <1g

Sodium 13mg

Alcohol has 7 calories per gram and counts as a fat rather than a carbohydrate if you are counting calories (a carbohydrate has 4 calories per gram).

Brunch

Country Brunch Casserole

The best brunch casserole—just prepare it the night before and have it ready to pop into the oven for a leisurely brunch.

Yield:
8 servings

Serving Size:
4 x 3-inch piece

Preparation Time:
15 minutes

Standing Time:
10 minutes

Cooking Time:
1 hour

½ c. chopped onion
2 T. water
Cooking spray
3 c. bread stuffing cubes
⅓ lb. Canadian bacon, thinly sliced, cut into bite-size pieces
1 c. (4 oz.) shredded reduced-fat sharp Cheddar cheese
3 eggs
2 egg whites
2 c. skim milk
½ tsp. dry mustard
½ tsp. onion salt

Nutrition Analysis Per Serving:

Calories 241

Protein 16g

Carbohydrate 22g

Fat 10g

(Saturated Fat 4g)

Cholesterol 100mg

Fiber 2g

Sodium 651mg

Microwave onion and water on high for 2 minutes, stirring occasionally. Place stuffing cubes in bottom of a 12 x 8 x 2-inch baking dish that has been lightly coated with cooking spray. Sprinkle with onion, Canadian bacon, and cheese. In a separate bowl, mix eggs, egg whites, milk, and seasonings; pour over stuffing mixture. Cover and refrigerate overnight. Bake, uncovered, at 325° for 1 hour. Let stand 10 minutes before serving.

Canadian bacon contains less than half the fat found in cured bacon. Thinly diced, it is an excellent substitute for sausage and bacon in traditional brunch dishes.

Crustless Vegetable Cheese Pie

No crust to add calories!

Cooking spray
¼ lb. fresh mushrooms, sliced
1 small zucchini, cut into ½-inch pieces
1 small green pepper, finely chopped
1 lb. 1% cottage cheese
1 c. (4 oz.) shredded part-
skim mozzarella cheese
3 eggs, beaten
1 pkg. (10 oz.) frozen chopped
spinach, thawed
1 T. dried dillweed
¼ tsp. garlic salt
⅛ tsp. black pepper

Yield:
6 servings

Serving Size:
⅙ of 9-inch pie

Preparation Time:
20 minutes

Cooking Time:
45–50 minutes

Preheat oven to 350°. Lightly coat a large non-stick skillet with cooking spray. Add mushrooms, zucchini, and green pepper; sauté until soft. Drain any excess liquid and cool to lukewarm. Combine cheeses, eggs, spinach (with all water squeezed out), dill, and mushroom mixture. Season with garlic salt and pepper; mix well. Place mixture in a 9-inch pie pan lightly coated with cooking spray. Bake about 45–50 minutes, or until knife inserted into the center comes out clean. Remove from oven and let stand for 5 minutes before serving.

Frozen vegetables are blanched (submerged in boiling water) before they are frozen to destroy enzymes that might affect their flavor and texture.

Nutrition Analysis Per Serving:

Calories 172

Protein 19g

Carbohydrate 7g

Fat 7g

(Saturated 2g)

Cholesterol 109mg

Fiber 2g

Sodium 527mg

Frittata Primavera

A delightful egg dish to serve with Mountain Biker's Banana Muffins (p. 140) and fresh fruit.

Yield:
4 servings

Serving Size:
4 x 4-inch piece

Preparation Time:
20 minutes

Cooking Time:
45 minutes

Cooking spray
1 ½ c. fresh mushrooms, sliced
1 c. chopped onion
1 c. diced tomatoes
1 clove garlic, minced
1 can (14 oz.) quartered artichoke hearts, drained
1 pkg. (10 oz.) frozen spinach, thawed
3 whole eggs
3 egg whites
½ tsp. Italian seasoning
1 c. (4 oz.) grated reduced-fat sharp Cheddar cheese
Salt and black pepper to taste

Nutrition Analysis Per Serving:

Calories 252

Protein 21g

Carbohydrate 21g

Fat 10g

(Saturated 5g)

Cholesterol 179mg

Fiber 8g

Sodium 525mg

Preheat oven to 350°. Lightly coat a non-stick skillet with cooking spray. Add mushrooms, onion, tomato, and garlic; sauté until tender. Beat eggs, egg whites, and Italian seasoning lightly. Combine vegetable mixture, artichokes, spinach, eggs, and cheese; stir. Pour mixture into an 8 x 8 x 2-inch baking dish lightly coated with cooking spray. Bake 45 minutes or until firm.

Eggs are one of the best sources of protein because they contain all of the essential amino acids required by the human body.

Sunday Morning Skillet

This dish is almost a filling meal on its own and has four food groups represented in one dish. Serve it with a fruit salad for a meal straight from the Food Pyramid!

1 medium baked potato, cubed
2 T. chopped green pepper
2 T. chopped onion
¼ tsp. garlic salt
¼ tsp. hot pepper sauce
Freshly ground black pepper
1 tsp. margarine
2 eggs
2 egg whites
2 tsp. water
¼ c. (1 oz.) shredded part-
skim mozzarella cheese
1 tomato, sliced

Yield:
2 servings

Serving Size:
About 1 cup

Preparation Time:
5 minutes

Cooking Time:
5–7 minutes

Combine potato, green pepper, onion, garlic salt, hot pepper sauce, and black pepper to taste; sauté in margarine in a non-stick pan for 2 minutes. Beat eggs and egg whites with water; fold gently into potato mixture. Cook, stirring frequently, until softly set. Sprinkle with cheese; serve with sliced tomatoes.

A potato can be cooked quickly in a microwave oven by piercing the potato with a fork and cooking on high power for 4–6 minutes. Turn potato after the first 2–3 minutes.

Nutrition Analysis Per Serving:

Calories 248

Protein 16g

Carbohydrate 23g

Fat 10g

(Saturated 3g)

Cholesterol 212mg

Fiber 3g

Sodium 346mg

Breakfast Burritos

A quick breakfast when you're running late.

Yield:
20 servings

Serving Size:
1 burrito

Preparation Time:
10 minutes

Cooking Time:
15 minutes

1 T. canola oil
1 medium onion, chopped
1 bag (2 lb.) frozen O'Brien potatoes
8 eggs, beaten
4 egg whites
½ c. skim milk
1 can (7 oz.) chopped green chiles
1 c. your favorite picante sauce
20 flour tortillas, warmed
Salsa Fresca (p. 10)

In a large non-stick skillet, heat oil. Add onion and cook for 3–4 minutes. To onion, add potatoes and continue to stir until potatoes begin to brown. In a large bowl, combine eggs, egg whites, and milk; mix well. Pour egg mixture over browned potatoes, add green chiles; scramble until eggs are cooked. Assemble burritos by putting about ⅓ cup of mixture onto a warm tortilla, spoon picante sauce over each, and roll. Serve alone or with *Salsa Fresca*.

Hint: Breakfast burritos freeze well and can be defrosted by wrapping in a paper towel and microwaving at 50 percent power for 3 minutes each.

When buying flour tortillas, check the ingredient list and choose tortillas that contain vegetable oil, a heart-healthy, polyunsaturated fat. Tortillas made with lard are higher in saturated fat, and may be more damaging to the heart and its vessels.

Nutrition Analysis Per Serving:

Calories 217

Protein 7g

Carbohydrate 32g

Fat 6g

(Saturated 2g)

Cholesterol 85mg

Fiber 1g

Sodium 452mg

Tofu Breakfast Scramble

This recipe provides an easy and tasty way to add more soy-based foods to your diet.

1 lb. firm tofu, crumbled
1 tsp. olive oil
⅓ c. chopped red bell pepper
4 mushrooms, chopped
3 green onions, chopped
2 cloves garlic, minced
2 eggs, beaten
1 T. freshly grated Parmesan cheese
½ tsp. Italian seasoning
¼ tsp. salt
⅛ tsp. black pepper

Yield:
4 servings

Serving Size:
½ cup

Preparation Time:
15 minutes

Cooking Time:
15 minutes

Drain the tofu in a colander. Heat the olive oil in a large non-stick skillet until hot. Add the red pepper, mushrooms, green onions, and garlic. Sauté for 5 minutes or until the vegetables are tender. Combine the tofu, eggs, cheese, Italian seasoning, salt, and pepper in a bowl and mix well. Stir into the vegetable mixture. Cook over medium heat for 5–10 minutes or until the eggs are cooked through and of the desired consistency, stirring constantly. Serve immediately.

Tip: Spoon the tofu scramble into warm flour tortillas and serve with *Salsa Fresca,* (p. 10) for a Southwestern touch.

Soy products may reduce the risk of breast or prostate cancer, osteoporosis, or hot flashes. They are a cholesterol-free source of protein, and they have less saturated fat than poultry or meat. Thus, they may help reduce the risk of heart disease, too.

Nutrition Analysis Per Serving:

Calories 137

Protein 13g

Carbohydrate 6g

Fat 7g

(Saturated 2g)

Cholesterol 107mg

Fiber 1g

Sodium 249mg

Turkey Sausage

The flavor of sausage without the fat! You'll want to make an extra batch to freeze or have on hand to complement egg dishes.

Yield:
4 servings

Serving Size:
1 patty

Preparation Time:
5 minutes

Chilling Time:
1 hour

Cooking Time:
10 minutes

½ lb. lean ground turkey
1 egg white
1 tsp. Italian seasoning
½ tsp. fennel seed (optional)
⅛ tsp. salt

Combine all ingredients in a small bowl; mix well. Shape mixture into 4 patties and chill at least 1 hour. Lightly coat a large non-stick skillet with cooking spray; place over medium heat until hot. Cook patties 5 minutes on each side or until done. Drain cooked patties on paper towels; serve warm.

Nutrition Analysis Per Serving:

Calories 66

Protein 15g

Carbohydrate <1g

Fat 1g

(Saturated 0g)

Cholesterol 23mg

Fiber 0g

Sodium 134mg

In traditional breakfast sausage, about 76 percent of calories come from fat. This adjusted recipe derives only 15 percent of its calories from fat.

French Coffee Cake

An attractive bundt coffee cake that tastes wonderful by itself or drizzled with powdered sugar.

⅔ c. reduced-calorie margarine
1 ¼ c. sugar
3 egg whites
1 ½ tsp. vanilla
3 c. flour
1 ½ tsp. baking powder
1 tsp. baking soda
2 c. plain nonfat or lowfat yogurt

Filling:
¼ c. chopped walnuts
¼ c. packed brown sugar
¼ c. sugar
1 ½ tsp. cinnamon

Preheat oven to 350°. Cream margarine and sugar in a medium-sized bowl with an electric mixer. Add egg whites and vanilla; mix thoroughly. Combine flour, baking powder, and baking soda. Gradually add flour mixture to creamed mixture alternately with yogurt, beginning and ending with flour mixture. In a separate bowl, combine filling ingredients, mixing with a fork until crumbly. Pour ⅓ of the batter into a 12-cup bundt pan coated with cooking spray. Sprinkle with half of the nut filling. Repeat layers, ending with batter. Bake for 45 minutes. Cool completely in pan on wire rack; then turn out of the pan and serve.

Yield:
16 servings

Serving Size:
1 wedge (¹⁄₁₆ of cake)

Preparation Time:
20–25 minutes

Cooking Time:
45 minutes

Nutrition Analysis Per Serving:

Calories 233

Protein 5g

Carbohydrate 43g

Fat 5g

(Saturated 1g)

Cholesterol 1mg

Fiber 1g

Sodium 229mg

Rhubarb Coffee Cake

Serve the rhubarb version of this coffee cake for a refreshing dessert at a summer brunch. In the winter, substitute cranberries for a festive breakfast treat.

Yield:
12 servings

Serving Size:
4x2 ½-inch piece

Preparation Time:
15 minutes

Cooking Time:
40–50 minutes

½ c. packed brown sugar
⅓ c. margarine, softened
1 egg
1 c. flour
1 c. whole-wheat flour
1 tsp. baking soda
¼ tsp. salt
1 c. plain nonfat or lowfat yogurt
1 ½ c. chopped rhubarb, fresh or frozen

Topping:
⅓ c. packed brown sugar
¼ c. regular oats, uncooked
1 T. margarine, softened
1 tsp. cinnamon

Preheat oven to 350°. Cream together brown sugar, margarine, and egg. Stir together flours, baking soda, and salt; add to creamed mixture alternately with yogurt. Stir in fruit. Pour into a greased and floured 12 x 8 x 2-inch baking pan. Mix sugar, oats, margarine, and cinnamon until crumbly; sprinkle over batter. Bake for 40–50 minutes.

Nutrition Analysis Per Serving:

Calories 207

Protein 4g

Carbohydrate 34g

Fat 7g

(Saturated 1g)

Cholesterol 18mg

Fiber 2g

Sodium 248mg

Eating with regularity establishes a regimen that keeps the appetite under control. Skipping meals easily leads to overeating, because the body hungers for more food.

Cranberry-Orange Pancakes

Serve this favorite to a holiday crowd, or enjoy it anytime. It's a celebration all its own.

1 c. fresh cranberries, washed
½ c. orange juice
1 c. flour
1 c. whole-wheat flour
2 tsp. baking powder
½ tsp. baking soda
1 T. sugar
¼ tsp. salt
2 T. oil
3 eggs
1 c. skim milk
½ c. chopped walnuts (optional)
Cooking spray

Combine cranberries and orange juice in a small saucepan. Bring to a boil and simmer until cranberries are soft (about 5 minutes). Let cool. Combine all dry ingredients; set aside. In a large mixing bowl, beat together oil, eggs, and milk. Stir in dry ingredients; then stir in cranberry mixture. Pour ¼ cup batter onto a hot griddle lightly coated with cooking spray. Cook until bubbles start to burst on first side; then flip pancake and continue to cook until golden brown.

If you like cranberries year round, buy extra when they're in season. Double-wrap the bag with plastic wrap and freeze them. They will last up to nine months.

Yield:
8 servings

Serving Size:
3 pancakes

Preparation Time:
20 minutes

Cooking Time:
15–20 minutes

Nutrition Analysis Per Serving:

Calories 211

Protein 8g

Carbohydrate 31g

Fat 6g

(Saturated 1g)

Cholesterol 80mg

Fiber 3g

Sodium 316mg

Wild Blueberry Pancakes

Yield:
4 servings

Serving Size:
3 pancakes

Preparation Time:
10 minutes

Cooking Time:
15–20 minutes

Nutrition Analysis Per Serving:

Calories 198

Protein 9g

Carbohydrate 36g

Fat 2g

(*Saturated 1g*)

Cholesterol 55mg

Fiber 5g

Sodium 361mg

1 c. lowfat buttermilk or plain lowfat yogurt
1 egg
½ tsp. vanilla
1 c. whole-wheat flour
1 T. sugar
1 tsp. baking powder
½ tsp. baking soda
1 c. blueberries, washed and drained
Cooking spray

In a large bowl, combine buttermilk, egg, and vanilla. In a separate bowl, combine dry ingredients. Mix dry ingredients into bowl with liquid ingredients. Fold in blueberries. Pour ¼ cup of batter onto a hot non-stick skillet or griddle lightly coated with cooking spray. When bubbles begin to burst on first side, flip and cook other side of pancake until golden brown. Serve warm.

Over-mixed pancake batter can develop the gluten in the flour and cause the pancakes to be tough.

Oatmeal-Apple Griddle Cakes

These pancakes are the perfect welcoming for autumn's apple harvest. Serve them with a warm Honey Hug (p. 51), and send your favorite junior athlete on her way!

½ c. flour
2 T. sugar
1 tsp. baking powder
½ tsp. salt
1 ½ c. cooked oatmeal
1 egg
¾ c. skim milk
2 T. oil
1 c. finely chopped apple
Cooking spray

Yield:
4 servings

Serving Size:
3 pancakes

Preparation Time:
15 minutes

Cooking Time:
15–20 minutes

Sift together flour, sugar, baking powder, and salt; add remaining ingredients and stir until moistened. Pour ¼ cup batter onto a hot griddle lightly coated with cooking spray. When bubbles start to burst on first side, flip pancake and cook other side till golden brown.

Nutrition Analysis Per Serving:

Calories 255

Protein 7g

Carbohydrate 35g

Fat 10g

(Saturated 2g)

Cholesterol 54mg

Fiber 3g

Sodium 455mg

Breakfast is the most important meal of the day. It doesn't have to be elaborate, but it should be high in nutrition to get your day off to a healthy start.

Pumpkin-Oat Pancakes

This pancake is a Halloween favorite given to us by Wildwood Resources and Child Care Food Program. It is a fun way to get your child to eat more vegetables.

Yield:
4 servings

Serving Size:
2 pancakes

Preparation Time:
10 minutes

Cooking Time:
5–10 minutes

1 c. lowfat buttermilk
½ c. regular (not quick) oats, uncooked
½ c. skim milk
½ c. pumpkin, mashed and cooked
1 egg
1 egg white
1 T. canola oil
⅓ c. flour
⅓ c. whole-wheat flour
2 T. sugar
2 T. wheat germ
1 tsp. baking powder
½ tsp. baking soda
¼ tsp. cinnamon
Cooking spray

Nutrition Analysis Per Serving:

Calories 241

Protein 10g

Carbohydrate 37g

Fat 7g

(Saturated 1g)

Cholesterol 56mg

Fiber 4g

Sodium 236mg

Combine buttermilk and oats; let mixture stand for 15 minutes. Add milk, pumpkin, egg, egg white, and oil to the oat mixture; mix well. In a small bowl, combine the remaining ingredients; stir into pumpkin mixture until batter is smooth. Lightly coat a hot griddle with cooking spray. Pour about ¼ cup batter onto griddle. Cook until bubbles start to burst on first side; flip pancake and cook on other side.

Spicy Oat Pancakes

¾ c. regular oats, uncooked
¾ c. whole-wheat flour
1 ½ tsp. baking powder
¾ tsp. cinnamon
¼ tsp. ground ginger
¼ tsp. baking soda
1 egg
1 c. skim milk
2 T. oil
1 T. honey or molasses

In a bowl, combine oats, flour, baking powder, cinnamon, ginger, and baking soda. In another bowl, mix egg, milk, oil; and honey; mix until blended and smooth. Combine dry and liquid ingredients and stir just until blended. Coat hot griddle with cooking spray. Pour a scant ¼ cup of batter onto griddle. Cook until bubbles start to burst on first side; flip pancake and cook other side.

While putting all of your eggs in one basket was never a good idea, neither is taking them out of the egg carton. Eggs left uncovered in the refrigerator can absorb odors from the foods around them, and that can ruin their flavor.

Yield:
5 servings

Serving Size:
2 pancakes

Preparation Time:
5–10 minutes

Cooking Time:
4–5 minutes

Nutrition Analysis Per Serving:

Calories 216

Protein 8g

Carbohydrate 29g

Fat 8g

(Saturated 2g)

Cholesterol 43mg

Fiber 4g

Sodium 251mg

German Pancakes with Applesauce

Impressive to look at—easy to prepare.

Yield:
6 servings

Serving Size:
⅙ of pancake and
apples

Preparation Time:
5–10 minutes

Cooking Time:
20–25 minutes

2 T. margarine
2 eggs
1 egg white
¾ c. skim milk
¾ c. flour

Applesauce:
5 medium apples, peeled, quartered, and cored
3 T. water
2 T. to ⅓ c. brown sugar, packed
½ tsp. cinnamon
Dash nutmeg

Preheat oven to 425°. Put margarine in a large
oven-proof pan and set in oven. Mix batter while
margarine melts. Put eggs and egg white in blender
container and process at high speed for 1 minute.
While processing, pour in milk; slowly add flour.
Continue processing for 30 seconds. Remove
pan from oven, swirl melted margarine around
edges of pan, and pour batter into hot frying pan.
Return to oven and bake for 10 minutes; reduce
temperature to 350°; bake for 10–15 minutes, or
until puffy and golden brown. Serve with *Saucy
Apples* or sprinkle powdered sugar and fresh fruit.

Applesauce: In 2 ½-quart glass casserole, combine apples and water. Microwave on high,
covered, for 6–8 minutes or until soft. Add
sugar to taste and mix in cinnamon and nutmeg. If desired, process in batches in a blender
or food processor until smooth. Serve warm.

**Nutrition Analysis
Per Serving:**

Calories 215

Protein 6g

Carbohydrate 36g

Fat 6g

(Saturated 1g)

Cholesterol 71mg

Fiber 3g

Sodium 97mg

Pancakes and Cointreau Strawberries

This light pancake will soon be a favorite for a weekend treat.

2 c. sliced strawberries
2 T. Cointreau or orange-flavored liqueur
2 eggs, beaten
2 egg whites
1 ⅓ c. skim milk
2 T. oil
1 c. flour
½ tsp. salt
Cooking spray

Mix strawberries and Cointreau; set aside. Combine eggs, milk, and oil; add flour and salt. Stir with wire whisk to eliminate lumps. Lightly coat a small non-stick skillet with cooking spray. Place skillet over medium heat. Pour only enough batter into skillet to coat pan bottom. When batter is set and browned, flip pancake. Remove from skillet after both sides are light brown. Serve hot with Cointreau strawberry topping.

Yield:
4 servings

Serving Size:
3 pancakes

Preparation Time:
10 minutes

Cooking Time:
15–20 minutes

Nutrition Analysis Per Serving:

Calories 288

Protein 12g

Carbohydrate 36g

Fat 10g

(Saturated 1g)

Cholesterol 107mg

Fiber 2g

Sodium 397mg

Multi-Grain Waffles

These high-fiber waffles are delicious anytime of the day or night, especially when served with fresh raspberries.

Yield:
4 servings

Serving Size:
1 waffle

Preparation Time:
5 minutes

Cooking Time:
10 minutes

Cooking spray
1 c. whole-wheat pancake mix
½ c. uncooked oat bran or
regular oats, uncooked
1 c. skim milk
1 T. oil
1 egg white
1 tsp. cinnamon

Lightly coat a waffle iron with cooking spray; allow to preheat. Mix together pancake mix and oat bran; combine with remaining ingredients. Pour batter onto hot waffle iron. Bake until steaming stops. Lift waffle from iron with fork.

Variation: For a lighter waffle, beat egg white and fold into mixture.

Nutrition Analysis Per Serving:

Calories 186

Protein 9g

Carbohydrate 31g

Fat 5g

(Saturated 1g)

Cholesterol 5mg

Fiber 4g

Sodium 260mg

Oven-Baked French Toast

This all-time favorite breakfast will rouse even the soundest of Sunday sleepers. Who can resist the cinnamon aroma of French toast as it bakes in an oven?

Cooking spray
2 eggs, beaten
2 egg whites
½ c. skim milk
1 ½ T. orange juice
1 T. brown sugar
½ tsp. cinnamon
½ tsp. vanilla
8 slices (¾-inch thick) French bread
1 T. powdered sugar

Yield:
4 servings

Serving Size:
2 slices

Preparation Time:
10 minutes

Cooking Time:
10–13 minutes

Preheat oven to 425°. Coat a shallow baking pan with cooking spray; heat pan in oven for 5 minutes or until hot. Meanwhile, combine eggs, egg whites, milk, orange juice, sugar, cinnamon, and vanilla; beat well. Dip bread slices into egg mixture, turning to coat evenly. Place dipped bread in hot pan. Bake for 5–7 minutes; turn and bake an additional 5–6 minutes until golden brown. Serve immediately with powdered sugar sprinkled on top.

This recipe for French toast can also be cooked on top of the stove in a non-stick skillet lightly coated with cooking spray.

Nutrition Analysis Per Serving:

Calories 257

Protein 12g

Carbohydrate 41g

Fat 5g

(Saturated 1g)

Cholesterol 106mg

Fiber 2g

Sodium 470mg

Fruit Kabobs with Honey Yogurt

Yield:
8 servings

Serving Size:
1 skewer

Preparation Time:
10 minutes

1 pt. whole strawberries, cleaned
1 cantaloupe, halved, seeded, cut
from rind into 1-inch cubes
2 kiwi, quartered and cut from rind
1 ½ c. pineapple, cut in 1-inch sections
1 container (8 oz.) lowfat
honey-vanilla yogurt

Thread fruit onto skewers; chill.
Serve with yogurt as a dip.

**Nutrition Analysis
Per Serving:**

Calories 106

Protein 3g

Carbohydrate 24g

Fat 1g

(Saturated <1g)

Cholesterol 2mg

Fiber 3g

Sodium 32mg

*Two average-size kiwis have more potassium
than a 6-inch banana, more dietary fiber than
a ⅔-cup serving of bran flakes, nearly twice as
much vitamin C as an orange, and twice the
vitamin E of an avocado—and only 90 calories.*

Hot Backpack Muesli

A hearty, warm breakfast for hiking the backcountry.

1 c. regular oats, uncooked
1 c. shredded whole-wheat cereal, crushed
¼ c. raisins
¼ c. unsweetened dried coconut
¼ c. chopped dried apples
¼ c. nuts or seeds
⅔ c. nonfat dry milk powder
1 tsp. cinnamon
3 c. water

Mix dry ingredients in a plastic bag for camping. In the evening, add 3 cups of water, cover mixture, and soak all night. In the morning, heat to boiling over the fire. Add more nonfat dry milk if desired.

When you can, use regular oats. Unlike quick oats, they still contain the whole grain—including the fiber.

Yield:
4 servings

Serving Size:
1 cup

Preparation Time:
7 minutes

Cooking Time:
5 minutes

Nutrition Analysis Per Serving:

Calories 57

Protein 4g

Carbohydrate 10g

Fat <1g

(Saturated <1g)

Cholesterol 2mg

Fiber 0g

Sodium 65mg

Simply Cappuccino

This recipe, obtained from the Western Dairy Council, is better than the cappuccinos from the best coffeehouses. That's why we put our name on it!

Yield:
4 servings

Serving Size:
1 cup

Preparation Time:
5 minutes

2 c. skim milk
1 T. sugar
2 c. freshly brewed strong coffee
Cinnamon to taste

Microwave skim milk on high for 2 minutes and 20 seconds. Pour into a blender container. Add sugar. Process at high speed for 1 minute or until frothy. Pour equal portions of the coffee into 4 mugs. Top each serving with some of the frothy milk. Sprinkle with cinnamon. Serve immediately.

Nutrition Analysis Per Serving:

Calories 57

Protein 4g

Carbohydrate 10g

Fat <1g

(Saturated <1g)

Cholesterol 2mg

Fiber 0g

Sodium 65mg

Honey Hug

Children can enjoy making this treat. It is the perfect drink after a day of sledding.

2 c. lowfat milk
2 tsp. honey
1 tsp. vanilla
Cinnamon

Heat milk over low heat; stir in honey and vanilla. To serve, pour into two mugs and sprinkle with cinnamon.

Yield:
2 servings

Serving Size:
1 cup

Preparation Time:
1 minute

Cooking Time:
3 minutes

Nutrition Analysis Per Serving:

Calories 151

Protein 8g

Carbohydrate 17g

Fat 5g

(Saturated 3g)

Cholesterol 20mg

Fiber 0g

Sodium 100mg

Orange Smoothie

Yield:
4 servings

Serving Size:
⅔ cup

Preparation Time:
3 minutes

1 can (6 oz.) frozen orange juice concentrate
1 c. lowfat milk
½ c. cold water
½ tsp. vanilla
10 ice cubes

Place all ingredients in a blender. Process until frothy and smooth. Serve immediately.

Nutrition Analysis Per Serving:

Calories 100

Protein 3g

Carbohydrate 19g

Fat 1g

(Saturated 1g)

Cholesterol 5mg

Fiber <1g

Sodium 28mg

The average American doesn't get enough calcium. Make sure that every day you consume calcium-rich foods such as lowfat dairy products and green leafy vegetables.

Berry Breakfast Shake

A tasty brunch drink with no extra sweeteners.

1 c. cold skim or lowfat milk
1 banana, frozen (or fresh
banana and ½ c. ice)
¼ c. frozen raspberries or
other frozen berries

Combine all ingredients in blender
and process until smooth.

Hint: If you freeze bananas without
peels, they will be much easier to use.

Yield:
1 serving

Serving Size:
1 ½ cups

Preparation Time:
3–5 minutes

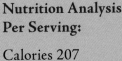

**Nutrition Analysis
Per Serving:**

Calories 207

Protein 10g

Carbohydrate 43g

Fat 1g

(Saturated <1g)

Cholesterol 4mg

Fiber 5g

Sodium 128mg

Palisade Peach Smoothie

A delicious treat anytime!

Yield:
1 serving

Serving Size:
2 cups

Preparation Time:
3 minutes

1 c. peach nonfat or lowfat yogurt
¾ c. peach nectar
1 ½ c. frozen sliced unsweetened peaches
½ c. frozen unsweetened raspberries

Combine the yogurt and peach nectar in a blender. Process until blended. Add the peaches and raspberries. Process until smooth. Serve immediately.

Nutrition Analysis Per Serving:

Calories 478

Protein 11g

Carbohydrate 105g

Fat 2g

(Saturated <1g)

Cholesterol 5mg

Fiber 13g

Sodium 130mg

Soups & Stews

Glenwood Gazpacho

This delicious, cool soup is perfect for a hot summer day.

Yield:
8 servings

Serving Size:
1 cup

Preparation Time:
20 minutes

Chilling Time:
Overnight

3 large tomatoes, chopped
1 bell pepper, chopped
1 cucumber, chopped
1 c. chopped celery
½ c. chopped onion
4 c. vegetable juice or tomato juice
5 T. red wine vinegar
½ tsp. black pepper

Combine all ingredients in a large non-metallic bowl. Chill overnight.

Nutrition Analysis Per Serving:

Calories 50

Protein 2g

Carbohydrate 10g

Fat <1g

(Saturated <1g)

Cholesterol 0mg

Fiber 2g

Sodium 327mg

The sodium content of this soup can be lowered by using two cups low-sodium vegetable juice and two cups regular vegetable juice.

Chilled Cucumber-Herb Soup

1 large cucumber
1 c. lowfat buttermilk
½ c. plain nonfat or lowfat yogurt
2 T. tarragon vinegar
2 cloves garlic, minced
1 tsp. Dijon mustard
3 leaves fresh basil, chopped
¼ tsp. dried whole tarragon
Salt and white pepper to taste

Scrub cucumber to remove any wax, but do not peel. Coarsely grate cucumber and drain. In a large bowl, combine cucumber and remaining ingredients. Chill to allow flavors to blend. Serve garnished with a sprig of parsley.

Are you hot and cold when it comes to soup? Try thinking of it as the perfect remedy when the thermometer's at one extreme or the other: Hot soup warms you up; cold soup cools you down. Soup really is that versatile.

Yield:
4 servings

Serving Size:
⅔ cup

Preparation Time:
10 minutes

Chilling Time:
1 hour

Nutrition Analysis Per Serving:

Calories 49

Protein 4g

Carbohydrate 8g

Fat 1g

(Saturated <1g)

Cholesterol 3mg

Fiber 1g

Sodium 113mg

Carrot-Cashew Soup

Serve with Quick Yeast Rolls (p. 132) and a salad for a cozy meal at home.

Yield:
6 servings

Serving Size:
1 cup

Preparation Time:
10–15 minutes

Cooking Time:
1 hour

4 c. grated carrots
1 c. chopped onions
2 T. canola oil
6 c. chicken stock
1 can (6 oz.) tomato paste
1 c. chopped apples
⅓ c. brown rice, uncooked
⅓ c. cashews
½ c. raisins (optional)

In a large pot, sauté carrots and onions in oil until vegetables are soft but not browned. Stir in stock, tomato paste, and apples, and bring the mixture to a boil. Stir in brown rice, reduce heat to a simmer, cover, and cook for 45 minutes or until rice is tender. Right before serving, stir in cashews and raisins (if desired).

Nutrition Analysis Per Serving:

Calories 217

Protein 7g

Carbohydrate 29g

Fat 9g

(Saturated 1g)

Cholesterol 0mg

Fiber 5g

Sodium 458mg

Studies show that those who start meals with hot soup eat fewer calories than those who skip the soup course.

Easy Tortilla Soup

Try this soup for an easy, zippy lunch.

**1 can (10 ½ oz.) low-sodium
chicken and rice soup
1 can (10 oz.) diced tomatoes and green chiles
12 baked tortilla chips**

In a saucepan, combine soup and tomatoes with
green chiles. Bring to a boil. Place tortilla chips
in the bottom of two soup bowls; pour the
soup mixture over them. Serve immediately.

Yield:
2 servings

Serving Size:
1 ¼ cups

Preparation Time:
2 minutes

Cooking Time:
5 minutes

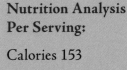

**Nutrition Analysis
Per Serving:**

Calories 153

Protein 4g

Carbohydrate 28g

Fat 3g

(Saturated 1g)

Cholesterol 7mg

Fiber 3g

Sodium 1190mg

Mexican Tomato Soup with Lime

A fun and enticing version of tomato soup.

Yield:
6 servings

Serving Size:
1 cup

Preparation Time:
10 minutes

Cooking Time:
12 minutes

1 ½ tsp. canola oil
3 cloves garlic, minced
2 tsp. cumin
1 can (46 oz.) tomato juice
2 c. chopped fresh tomatoes
¼ c. fresh lime juice
1 tsp. dried basil
Hot pepper sauce to taste
20 baked tortilla chips

Heat the canola oil in a large saucepan over low heat. Add the garlic and cumin. Cook for 1 minute, stirring constantly; do not brown. Stir in the tomato juice, tomatoes, lime juice, basil, and hot pepper sauce. Simmer for 10 minutes, stirring occasionally. Crush the tortilla chips into 6 soup bowls. Ladle the soup over the tortilla chips.

Nutrition Analysis Per Serving:

Calories 83

Protein 3g

Carbohydrate 17g

Fat 2g

(Saturated <1g)

Cholesterol 0mg

Fiber 2g

Sodium 817mg

Tomatoes and tomato products are rich in the antioxidants vitamins A and C, as well as lycopene, a phytochemical that gives them their red color. Eating plenty of tomatoes—especially tomato soups, sauces, and juices—could substantially decrease the risk for developing a variety of cancers.

Autumn Curry Soup

Seasonings give this soup an appealing sweetness, and canned pumpkin makes the preparation quick.

1 T. vegetable oil
⅓ c. chopped onion
1 clove garlic, crushed
1 tsp. curry powder
¼ tsp. coriander
3 c. chicken broth
2 c. canned pumpkin
Salt and black pepper to taste

Heat the oil in a saucepan until hot. Add the onion and garlic. Sauté until the onion is tender. Stir in the curry powder and coriander and cook for 1 minute, stirring frequently. Stir in the broth and pumpkin. Bring to a boil, stirring occasionally. Pour the pumpkin mixture into a blender or food processor. Process until puréed. Season with salt and pepper and ladle into soup bowls. Serve immediately.

Variation: Try substituting butternut squash for the pumpkin.

Yield:
6 servings

Serving Size:
1 cup

Preparation Time:
15 minutes

Cooking Time:
10 minutes

Nutrition Analysis Per Serving:

Calories 71

Protein 4g

Carbohydrate 8g

Fat 3g

(Saturated <1g)

Cholesterol 0mg

Fiber 4g

Sodium 392mg

Boulder Black Bean Soup

This is the perfect supper after an awesome day of skiing!

Yield:
8 servings

Serving Size:
1 cup

Preparation Time:
15 minutes

Cooking Time:
25–35 minutes

2 tsp. olive oil
1 medium onion, chopped
3 cloves garlic, minced
1 tsp. dried oregano leaves
½ tsp. dried thyme leaves
½ tsp. cumin
¼ tsp. cayenne pepper
3 c. canned black beans, rinsed and drained
3 c. low-sodium chicken broth
2 tomatoes, chopped
½ c. chopped onion (optional)
½ c. shredded, reduced-fat Monterey
Jack cheese (optional)

Nutrition Analysis Per Serving:

Calories 94

Protein 6g

Carbohydrate 18g

Fat 2g

(Saturated <1g)

Cholesterol 0mg

Fiber 6g

Sodium 225mg

Heat oil in a large saucepan over medium heat. Sauté onion and garlic until tender (about 5 minutes). Stir in oregano, thyme, cumin, and pepper; cook one minute longer. Place half of beans in a blender and purée until smooth, adding chicken broth as needed to make a smooth purée. Add purée, remaining whole beans, and broth to saucepan. Bring to a boil over medium heat; then simmer uncovered for 20–30 minutes. Serve garnished with diced tomatoes, and if desired, onion and shredded cheese.

Savory Seven-Bean Soup

Bags of this bean mixture with a copy of this recipe make a wonderful gift.

2 c. bean mixture (see below), rinsed
8 c. water
1 large onion, chopped
1 lb. lean ham, diced
1 can (10 oz.) diced tomatoes and green chiles
1 clove garlic, minced
1 can (16 oz.) whole tomatoes, undrained
Juice of 1 lemon

**Bean Mixture (use equal amounts
of the dried beans listed):**
Green split peas
Yellow split peas
Red beans
Black-eyed peas
Pinto beans
Great Northern beans
Lentils

Combine 2 cups of bean mixture, water,
onion, and ham in a 5-quart slow cooker;
simmer on low setting for 6 hours,
stirring occasionally. Add remaining
ingredients and simmer for 1 hour more.

*Beans are one of the best sources of both
soluble and insoluble fiber. While soluble fiber
may be helpful in reducing blood cholesterol
levels, insoluble fiber may be helpful in
preventing some forms of colon cancer.*

Yield:
10 servings

Serving Size:
1 ¼ cups

Preparation Time:
15 minutes

Cooking Time:
7 hours

**Nutrition Analysis
Per Serving:**

Calories 213

Protein 20g

Carbohydrate 28g

Fat 3g

(Saturated 1g)

Cholesterol 14mg

Fiber 6g

Sodium 718mg

"No-Hassle" Split Pea Soup

Serve with Mexican Cornbread (p. 135) for a cold-weather evening.

Yield:
8 servings

Serving Size:
1 cup

Soaking Time:
Overnight

Preparation Time:
20 minutes

Cooking Time:
6–10 hours

1 lb. dry green split peas (soaked overnight and drained)
1 qt. water
¾ lb. lean ham, cubed
½ T. onion powder
¼ tsp. pepper
½ c. chopped celery
1 c. sliced carrots
1 medium onion, chopped
1 bay leaf (optional)

Put all ingredients into a slow cooker. Cover and cook on low for 10–12 hours or on high for 5–6 hours.

Nutrition Analysis Per Serving:

Calories 275

Protein 24g

Carbohydrate 41g

Fat 2g

(Saturated 1g)

Cholesterol 20mg

Fiber 1g

Sodium 620mg

Switching from bacon to lean ham in recipes saves 1,499 calories and 148 grams of fat. Twelve ouncs of bacon contains 1,995 calories and 166.8 grams of fat; twelve ounces of lean ham contains 496 calories and 18.8 grams of fat.

Creamy Potato Soup

1 lb. (3 medium) potatoes,
peeled and thinly sliced
1 ½ c. low-sodium chicken broth
1 c. skim milk
2 tsp. margarine or butter
⅓ c. chopped green onion
2 T. chopped fresh parsley
½ tsp. celery seed
¼ tsp. dried whole tarragon
⅛ tsp. black pepper
Salt to taste

Combine potatoes and broth in a 2-quart saucepan. Bring to a boil; cover and cook until potatoes are tender (about 10 minutes). Cool slightly. Pour into blender and blend until smooth; return to saucepan. Stir in milk, margarine, onions, parsley, celery seed, tarragon, and pepper. Bring to a boil; stir in salt. Serve warm or cold, thinned with a little additional milk.

Yield:
4 servings

Serving Size:
1 cup

Preparation Time:
20 minutes

Cooking Time:
20 minutes

Nutrition Analysis Per Serving:

Calories 135

Protein 7g

Carbohydrate 25g

Fat 3g

(Saturated 1g)

Cholesterol 1mg

Fiber 3g

Sodium 84mg

Velvet Corn Chowder

Yield:
4 servings

Serving Size:
1 cup

Preparation Time:
15–20 minutes

Cooking Time:
15–20 minutes

2 cans (10 ½ oz. each) low-sodium chicken broth
2 egg whites
2 T. skim milk
1 can (8 ¾ oz.) cream-style corn
2 T. cold water
1 T. cornstarch
¼ c. finely chopped lean ham
Paprika to taste

Bring chicken broth to a boil over high heat. Beat egg whites and milk until frothy and set aside. Add corn to broth and bring to a boil; reduce heat. Mix water and cornstarch; add to soup and cook, stirring until thickened. Turn off heat and add egg white; stir quickly once. Add the ham; garnish with paprika and serve immediately.

Nutrition Analysis Per Serving:

Calories 103

Protein 8g

Carbohydrate 16g

Fat 2g

(Saturated <1g)

Cholesterol 3mg

Fiber 1g

Sodium 341mg

Cutting calories is one way to shed pounds. Burning calories counts, too! The best approach is to decrease calories and increase physical activity.

Cheddar-Chicken Chowder

This delicious chowder is hearty enough to be an entrée.

1 lb. boneless, skinless chicken breasts
1 c. chopped onion
1 c. chopped red bell pepper
2 cloves garlic, mined
2 tsp. olive oil
4 ½ c. fat-free chicken broth
1 ¾ c. chopped red potatoes
2 ¼ c. frozen whole kernel corn
2 c. skim milk
½ c. flour
**¾ c. (3 oz.) shredded, reduced-
fat sharp Cheddar cheese**
½ tsp. salt
¼ tsp. black pepper

Yield:
7 servings

Serving Size:
1 cup

Preparation Time:
15 minutes

Cooking Time:
45 minutes

Cut the chicken into bite-size pieces. Sauté the chicken, onion, red pepper, and garlic in the olive oil in a large skillet for 5 minutes. Stir in the broth and red potatoes. Bring to a boil; reduce heat. Simmer, covered, for 20 minutes or until the potatoes are tender, stirring occasionally. Add the corn and mix well.

In a medium-sized bowl, whisk the skim milk into the flour until blended. Add to the chicken mixture gradually, whisking constantly. Cook over medium heat for 15 minutes or until thickened, stirring frequently. Stir in the cheese, salt, and pepper. Ladle into soup bowls.

**Nutrition Analysis
Per Serving:**

Calories 279

Protein 26g

Carbohydrate 32g

Fat 6g

(Saturated 2g)

Cholesterol 44mg

Fiber 3g

Sodium 533mg

Seafood Chowder

Yield:
8 servings

Serving Size:
1 cup

Preparation Time:
25 minutes

Cooking Time:
40 minutes

Nutrition Analysis Per Serving:

Calories 224

Protein 25g

Carbohydrate 12g

Fat 6g

(Saturated 1g)

Cholesterol 75mg

Fiber 3g

Sodium 756mg

1 large onion, chopped
1 large green bell pepper, chopped
2 large ribs celery, chopped
2 cloves garlic, minced
1 T. olive oil
2 cans (14 oz. each) chopped tomatoes, undrained
2 cans (8 oz. each) tomato sauce
1 c. white wine
2 T. parsley flakes
1 tsp. dried basil
½ tsp. dried oregano leaves
1 bay leaf
1 lb. crabmeat, flaked
1 lb. whitefish, cubed
Cayenne pepper to taste

Sauté the onion, green pepper, celery, and garlic in the olive oil in a medium stockpot until the vegetables are tender. Add the undrained tomatoes, tomato sauce, wine, parsley flakes, basil, oregano, and bay leaf, and mix well. Cook for 20–30 minutes, stirring occasionally. Stir in the crabmeat and whitefish. Cook for 10 minutes longer or until the fish is cooked through, stirring occasionally. Stir in cayenne pepper. Discard the bay leaf. Ladle over hot rice in soup bowls.

Do not store uncooked fish in the refrigerator for more than 24 hours. Uncooked poultry or ground beef can be stored in the refrigerator for 1–2 days and other uncooked meats for 3–5 days.

Southwestern Stew

1 T. canola oil
2 lbs. boneless pork shoulder or
sirloin, cut into 1 ½-inch cubes
2 c. chopped onion
1 c. chopped green bell pepper
2 cloves garlic, minced
2–3 T. chili powder
2 tsp. dried oregano leaves
¼ tsp. salt
2 cans (14 ½ oz. each) low-
sodium chicken broth
3 c. chopped potatoes, peeled
and cut into 1-inch cubes
1 pkg. (10 oz.) frozen corn
1 can (15 ½ oz.) garbanzo beans, drained

Yield:
8 servings

Serving Size:
1 ¼ cups

Preparation Time:
30 minutes

Cooking Time:
1 ¾ hours

Heat oil in a large pot. Add pork and brown over medium-high heat; drain fat. Stir in onions, green pepper, garlic, seasonings, and chicken broth. Cover; cook over medium-low heat for 50–60 minutes, or until pork is tender. Add potatoes, corn, and beans. Cover and cook 20–30 minutes longer.

**Nutrition Analysis
Per Serving:**

Calories 341

Protein 30g

Carbohydrate 33g

Fat 11g

(Saturated 3g)

Cholesterol 74mg

Fiber 6g

Sodium 355mg

To remove fat from soup, cover and chill it overnight or until the fat solidifies on the surface of the soup. Then lift it off and discard it.

Miner's Beef Stew

A slow-cooked stew with a mouth-watering aroma.

Yield:
6 servings

Serving Size:
1 ½ cups

Preparation Time:
20 minutes

Cooking Time:
8–10 hours

2 lbs. lean top-round steak,
cut into 1-inch cubes
¼ c. flour
1 T. canola oil
3 lbs. frozen or fresh stew vegetables
1 c. beef broth
1 T. dried parsley flakes
3 cloves garlic, minced
1 tsp. Worcestershire sauce
½ tsp. dried thyme or marjoram
¼ tsp. salt
¼ tsp. black pepper

Combine meat and flour in a sealable plastic
bag; close bag and shake well. Heat oil in a
large non-stick skillet over high heat. Add flour-
coated meat and cook until browned, stirring
often. Place browned meat, stew vegetables,
and remaining ingredients into slow cooker.
Stir just enough to mix spices. Cover and cook
on low for 8–10 hours (high 4–5 hours).

Nutrition Analysis Per Serving:

Calories 371

Protein 38g

Carbohydrate 34g

Fat 8g

(Saturated 2g)

Cholesterol 86mg

Fiber 2g

Sodium 454mg

*Stew vegetables can be found frozen,
or sometimes even bagged together
fresh in the produce department.*

Claim-Jumper's Black Bean Stew

2 tsp. olive oil
1 large red onion, chopped
1 can (15 oz.) black beans, drained and rinsed
1 can (16 oz.) stewed tomatoes, undrained
3 T. dried parsley flakes
½ tsp. coriander
¼ tsp. garlic powder
4 c. cooked rice
1 ⅓ T. Parmesan cheese, grated

In a large non-stick skillet, heat oil; add onion and sauté until transparent. Add beans and remaining ingredients except rice and Parmesan cheese; bring to a boil. Reduce heat and simmer for 20 minutes to allow flavors to blend. Serve over hot rice and sprinkle with Parmesan cheese.

Yield:
4 servings

Serving Size:
1 ¾ cups

Preparation Time:
15 minutes

Cooking Time:
20 minutes

Nutrition Analysis Per Serving:

Calories 342

Protein 11g

Carbohydrate 71g

Fat 3g

(Saturated 1g)

Cholesterol 1mg

Fiber 7g

Sodium 453mg

Winter Stew

Try this soup as soon as the snow falls!

Yield:
12 servings

Serving Size:
1 cup

Preparation Time:
15–20 minutes

Cooking Time:
4–6 hours

1 lb. lean ground beef
1 small head cabbage, cored
and cut in small wedges
1 small onion, chopped
1 c. chopped celery
1 c. chopped carrots
1 c. chopped zucchini
1 c. chopped turnip
1 can (46 oz.) vegetable juice
1 c. brown rice, barley, or bulgur
Black pepper, to taste

Brown ground beef; drain fat. Place in slow cooker, top with vegetables, cover with vegetable juice, and season with pepper. Cook for 4–6 hours on low. Add rice, barley, or bulgur and cook 1 hour longer or until grain is cooked (allow 1 ½ hours to cook if using rice).

Nutrition Analysis Per Serving:

Calories 175

Protein 11g

Carbohydrate 23g

Fat 4g

(Saturated 2g)

Cholesterol 25mg

Fiber 3g

Sodium 358mg

Brown rice takes twice as long to cook as white rice. So, if time is limited, try quick-cooking brown rice.

Lentil Stew

This recipe comes from the Date Bar restaurant in Colorado Springs.

1 pkg. (16 oz.) lentils
10 c. water
1 onion, chopped
½ c. rice
2 tsp. salt
2 cloves garlic, minced
1 tsp. dried oregano leaves
1 tsp. dried parsley flakes
3 large tomatoes, chopped
1 carrot, chopped
1 pkg. (10 oz.) frozen chopped
spinach, thawed and drained

Yield:
10 servings

Serving Size:
1 ¼ cups

Preparation Time:
30 minutes

Cooking Time:
45 minutes

Wash and sort lentils; drain well. In a large pot, combine lentils, water, onion, rice, salt, garlic, oregano, and parsley; bring to a boil. Cover and simmer for 25 minutes. Add tomatoes, carrot, and spinach. Simmer 20 minutes or until lentils are tender.

Nutrition Analysis Per Serving:

Calories 212

Protein 15g

Carbohydrate 39g

Fat 1g

(Saturated <1g)

Cholesterol 0mg

Fiber 16g

Sodium 503mg

If legumes, such as lentils, are not stored in a cool, dry place, they sometimes develop "hard-shell." When this occurs, it is difficult to re-hydrate them and usually requires excessive cooking.

Hearty White Chili

A new version of an old favorite that is sure to please traditional chili fans.

Yield:
6 servings

Serving Size:
1 cup

Preparation Time:
10 minutes

Cooking Time:
70 minutes

1 lb. boneless, skinless chicken breasts
1 medium yellow onion, chopped
1 T. olive oil
1 can (4 oz.) chopped green chiles, drained
3 cloves garlic, minced
1 tsp. cumin
¾ tsp. dried oregano leaves
⅛ tsp. cayenne pepper
1 can (16 oz.) cannellini beans, drained and rinsed
2 cans (16 oz.) low-sodium chicken broth
½ c. shredded Monterey Jack cheese

Cut the chicken into bite-size pieces. Sauté the chicken and onion in olive oil in a large saucepan until the chicken is white and the onion is tender. Stir in the chiles, garlic, cumin, oregano, and cayenne pepper. Sauté for 2 minutes. Add the beans and broth and mix well. Bring to a boil; reduce heat. Simmer for 45–60 minutes or until of the desired consistency, stirring occasionally. Ladle into chili bowls. Sprinkle with cheese.

Nutrition Analysis Per Serving:

Calories 232

Protein 23g

Carbohydrate 15g

Fat 8g

(Saturated 3g)

Cholesterol 53mg

Fiber 4g

Sodium 553mg

Skier's Vegetable Chili

With a food processor, this superb chili is a cinch to prepare.

1 c. chopped onion
½ c. diced green bell pepper
2 T. olive oil
2 cloves garlic, minced
2 c. chopped zucchini
1 c. chopped carrots
2 cans (15 oz. each) pinto or kidney beans, drained and rinsed
2 cans (16 oz. each) diced tomatoes, undrained
2 T. chili powder
¼ tsp. cumin
1 tsp. Italian seasoning
Black pepper to taste
½ c. water

In a 4-quart saucepan, sauté onion and green pepper in olive oil over medium-low heat until onions are soft (about 8 minutes). Add garlic; stir in zucchini and carrots. Cook over low heat for 2 minutes. To vegetable mixture, add beans, tomatoes, chili powder, cumin, Italian seasoning, pepper, and water; stir. Bring mixture to a boil; reduce heat and simmer for about 35–45 minutes.

Yield:
8 servings

Serving Size:
1 cup

Preparation Time:
25 minutes

Cooking Time:
1 hour

Nutrition Analysis Per Serving:

Calories 208

Protein 10g

Carbohydrate 35g

Fat 4g

(Saturated 1g)

Cholesterol 0mg

Fiber 13g

Sodium 187mg

Gringo Chili

Whip this recipe up in minutes when the urge for a spicy chili strikes you.

Yield:
6 servings

Serving Size:
1 ¼ cups

Preparation Time:
10–15 minutes

Cooking Time:
15–20 minutes

1 lb. lean ground turkey
1 medium onion, chopped
2 cloves garlic, minced
1 can (32 oz.) diced tomatoes, undrained
1 can (15 oz.) pinto or kidney beans, drained
1 can (6 oz.) tomato paste
½ c. green chili salsa
1 T. chili powder

In a large non-stick skillet, cook turkey, onion, and garlic over medium heat until turkey loses its pink color; drain excess fat. Stir in remaining ingredients; bring to boil. Cover, reduce heat, and simmer 15–20 minutes.

Nutrition Analysis Per Serving:

Calories 237

Protein 27g

Carbohydrate 31g

Fat 2g

(Saturated <1g)

Cholesterol 30mg

Fiber 8g

Sodium 560mg

Green Chili

This recipe is a favorite among Mexican food lovers.

Cooking spray
1 medium onion, chopped
2 cloves garlic, minced
½ tsp. cumin
¼ tsp. black pepper
⅛ tsp. dried oregano leaves
3 medium boiling potatoes, cleaned
and cut into small cubes
1 can (7 oz.) chopped green chiles
1 can (49 ½ oz.) chicken broth (about 6 cups)
3 oz. shredded reduced-fat
Monterey Jack cheese

Yield:
6 servings

Serving Size:
1 ½ cups

Preparation Time:
20 minutes

Cooking Time:
1 hour

Lightly coat a 2-quart saucepan with cooking spray; add onion and garlic and sauté over medium heat for about 5 minutes, until onion wilts. Stir in cumin and pepper; continue to cook 2–3 minutes or until onion starts to show signs of browning. Add oregano, potatoes, green chiles, and chicken broth. Bring to a boil; cover and simmer 45 minutes. Serve hot with cheese sprinkled evenly over each serving.

Instead of margarine, butter, or oil, use non-stick cooking sprays. Margarine and oil provide 100–120 calories per tablespoon. There are only 6 calories per 2 ½ second-spray of cooking spray.

Nutrition Analysis Per Serving:

Calories 124

Protein 8g

Carbohydrate 18g

Fat 3g

(Saturated 2g)

Cholesterol 10mg

Fiber 4g

Sodium 612mg

Snowy Weekend Cassoulet

This soup will fill your house with a wonderful aroma.

Yield:
8 servings

Serving Size:
1 cup

Preparation Time:
20 minutes

Cooking Time:
1 hour and 20 minutes

Nutrition Analysis Per Serving:

Calories 308

Protein 32g

Carbohydrate 37g

Fat 4g

(Saturated Fat 1g)

Cholesterol 51mg

Fiber 11g

Sodium 727mg

¼ c. dried lentils
¼ c. dried split peas
2 quarts water
1 can (28 oz.) diced tomatoes, undrained
1 can (15 oz.) black beans, drained and rinsed
1 can (15 oz.) Great Northern beans, drained and rinsed
¼ c. barley
1 medium onion, chopped
2 ribs celery, chopped
½ large green bell pepper, chopped
2 cloves garlic, minced
¼ tsp. dried thyme leaves
red pepper to taste
2 boneless skinless chicken breast halves, cubed
7 oz. smoked reduced-fat sausage, sliced
1 c. chopped lean ham

Sort and rinse lentils and split peas. Combine the water, undrained tomatoes, beans, barley, onion, celery, green pepper, garlic, thyme, and red pepper in a stockpot and mix well. Simmer for 1 hour, stirring occasionally. Stir in chicken, sausage, and ham. Simmer until chicken is cooked through, stirring occasionally. Ladle into soup bowls.

Grate additional fresh vegetables when they are plentiful in the grocery or garden and store them in small portions in sealable freezer bags. The vegetables will be ready for adding to sauces and soups, muffins, breads, and desserts. An easy way to incorporate "five-a-day!"

SALADS

SALAD DRESSINGS

MAIN DISH SALADS

Breckenridge Broccoli Salad

A hit at potlucks!

Yield:
6 servings

Serving Size:
½ cup

Preparation Time:
15 minutes

3 c. broccoli florets
½ c. shredded, reduced-fat
sharp Cheddar cheese
½ c. sliced red onion
3 T. bacon bits

Dressing:
¾ c. light mayonnaise
3 T. sugar
1 ½ T. vinegar

Combine broccoli, cheese, onion, and bacon
bits. Mix mayonnaise, sugar, and vinegar
and toss with broccoli mixture. Serve
immediately or chill until time to eat.

**Nutrition Analysis
Per Serving:**

Calories 185

Protein 5g

Carbohydrate 13g

Fat 13g

(Saturated 3g)

Cholesterol 20mg

Fiber 1g

Sodium 443mg

*A serving of broccoli (about 1 cup) contains
more vitamin C than an orange—more
than enough to meet the recommended
dietary allowance for one day.*

Tangy Carrot-Raisin Salad

A delicious, nutrient-rich salad that will soon become a family favorite.

2 c. grated carrots
⅔ c. raisins
¼ c. peach- or orange-flavored lowfat yogurt
2 T. frozen orange juice concentrate

Combine carrots and raisins; set aside.
Blend yogurt and orange juice concentrate.
Combine salad and dressing; mix well.

Yield:
6 servings

Serving Size:
½ cup

Preparation Time:
10 minutes

If carrots and celery become limp, soak them in ice water. This will return some of the lost crispness by hydrating cells that have lost water during storage.

Nutrition Analysis Per Serving:

Calories 82

Protein 1g

Carbohydrate 20g

Fat <1g

(Saturated <1g)

Cholesterol 1mg

Fiber 2g

Sodium 32mg

Confetti Pasta Salad

Double this recipe for your next party!

Yield:
6 servings

Serving Size:
½ cup

Preparation Time:
20 minutes

Marinating Time:
2–4 hours

Nutrition Analysis Per Serving:

Calories 168

Protein 7g

Carbohydrate 24g

Fat 5g

(Saturated 1g)

Cholesterol 2mg

Fiber 2g

Sodium 388mg

2 c. corkscrew pasta, cooked and drained
1 ½ c. mushrooms, sliced
1 c. cherry tomatoes, halved
1 c. sliced zucchini
1 can (14 oz.) quartered artichoke hearts, drained
¼ c. green onions, chopped
⅔ c. lowfat Italian dressing
3 T. grated Parmesan cheese

In a large bowl, combine pasta and vegetables; cover with Italian dressing and marinate in refrigerator for several hours. Drain. Sprinkle cheese over pasta and vegetable mixture; toss lightly. Serve immediately or chill until serving time.

Garden Pasta Salad

1 pkg. (8–10 oz.) tri-color pasta, uncooked
3 carrots, sliced and quartered
1 cucumber, peeled and diced
6–8 radishes
1 c. broccoli florets
2 pkgs. dry light Italian dressing mix
½ c. vinegar
¼ c. water
Parmesan cheese, grated

Cook pasta according to package directions. Rinse under cold running water and drain; place in large bowl. Add vegetables and mix well. Prepare dressing using two packages of dry dressing mix, vinegar, and water; mix well. Pour dressing over salad. Let salad set in refrigerator for approximately 2 hours. Mix prior to serving and garnish with Parmesan cheese.

Using tri-colored pasta in recipes is a colorful, easy way to make pasta dishes look festive. The colors are derived from plant dyes and usually do not change the flavor or the nutritive content of the pasta.

Yield:
12 servings

Serving Size:
½ cup

Preparation Time:
30 minutes

Standing Time:
2 hours

Cooking Time:
10 minutes

Nutrition Analysis Per Serving:

Calories 88

Protein 3g

Carbohydrate 18g

Fat <1g

(Saturated <1g)

Cholesterol 0mg

Fiber 2g

Sodium 117mg

Sweet & Sour Pasta Salad

This versatile salad makes either a tangy side dish or a main dish salad when you add your favorite seafood or shellfish.

Yield:
10 servings

Serving Size:
1 cup

Preparation Time:
20 minutes

Chilling Time:
30 minutes

Nutrition Analysis Per Serving:

Calories 109

Protein 3g

Carbohydrate 21g

Fat 2g

(Saturated <1g)

Cholesterol 0mg

Fiber 2g

Sodium 107mg

1 ⅓ c. any shaped pasta, uncooked
1 can (15 oz.) unsweetened pineapple chunks, undrained
2 c. broccoli florets
1 c. chopped celery
1 c. frozen petite peas
½ c. chopped red bell pepper
¼ c. chopped green onion

Dressing:
⅓ c. white wine vinegar
2 T. Dijon mustard
2 T. honey
2 T. lemon juice
2 T. pineapple juice (from reserved juice)
1 T. olive oil
½ tsp. dried basil leaves
½ tsp. garlic powder

Cook pasta according to package directions. Drain pineapple chunks, reserving 2 tablespoons of juice for dressing. Mix dressing ingredients together. Combine all salad ingredients and toss with dressing. Chill; then serve.

Fresh Tomato-Tortellini Salad

Celebrate summer's crop of fresh tomatoes with this flavorful salad.

**1 pkg. (9 oz.) cheese tortellini
(frozen, refrigerated, or dry)
2 c. fresh, ripe tomatoes
3 large leaves of fresh basil
3 sprigs of fresh parsley
2 cloves garlic, minced
1 ½ T. olive oil
2 tsp. red wine vinegar
¼ tsp. salt
¼ tsp. freshly ground black pepper**

Cook tortellini according to package directions until tender. Meanwhile, dice the tomatoes in ¼-inch pieces; place in a large bowl. Finely chop basil and parsley. Add herbs and garlic to tomatoes. Gently stir in oil, vinegar, salt, and pepper. Drain tortellini and toss with tomato mixture to coat.

Yield:
10 servings

Serving Size:
½ cup

Preparation Time:
15 minutes

Cooking Time:
10 minutes

**Nutrition Analysis
Per Serving:**

Calories 104

Protein 4g

Carbohydrate 14g

Fat 4g

(Saturated 1g)

Cholesterol 11mg

Fiber 1g

Sodium 148mg

Jicama & Orange Salad

Served on a bed of greens, this makes a beautiful, refreshing salad.

Yield:
6 servings

Serving Size:
½ cup

Preparation Time:
5 minutes

Chilling Time:
20 minutes

1 can (11 oz.) mandarin orange segments, drained
2 c. julienne-cut jicama
2 T. orange juice
2 T. rice vinegar
1 tsp. olive oil

Combine oranges and jicama in a medium bowl. Mix together juice, vinegar, and oil. Pour dressing over orange and jicama mixture and chill.

Nutrition Analysis Per Serving:

Calories 44

Protein 1g

Carbohydrate 9g

Fat 1g

(Saturated <1g)

Cholesterol 0mg

Fiber 2g

Sodium 4mg

Jicama is a tropical root vegetable that resembles a giant turnip. The taste and texture is a cross between an apple and a water chestnut.

Asian Slaw

Ramen noodles and fresh cabbage lend a satisfying crispness to this slaw.

3 c. shredded cabbage
4 green onions, chopped
2 tsp. sesame seeds
**1 pkg. dry, lowfat chicken-
flavored Ramen noodles**
¼ c. water
3 T. sugar
2 T. oil
1 T. vinegar
⅓ c. slivered almonds, toasted (optional)

Toss cabbage, onion, sesame seeds, and dry
Ramen noodles together; set aside. Mix
water, sugar, oil, vinegar, and contents of
Ramen seasoning packet to make dressing.
Pour dressing over cabbage mixture; toss.
Sprinkle with toasted almonds, if desired.

*Look for reduced-fat Ramen noodles. Traditional
fried Ramen noodles are high in fat.*

Yield:
6 servings

Serving Size:
½ cup

Preparation Time:
15 minutes

**Nutrition Analysis
Per Serving:**

Calories 118

Protein 2g

Carbohydrate 16g

Fat 5g

(Saturated <1g)

Cholesterol 0mg

Fiber 1g

Sodium 202mg

Creamy Fruit Salad

Vanilla pudding and banana yogurt lend pizzazz to this pot-luck favorite.

Yield:
10 servings

Serving Size:
½ cup

Preparation Time:
5 minutes

Chilling Time:
30 minutes

1 can (11 oz.) mandarin oranges, drained
1 can (20 oz.) pineapple chunks, drained
3 bananas, sliced
2 red apples, chopped

Fruit Sauce:
1 box (1.3 oz.) sugar-free,
instant vanilla pudding
1 c. skim milk
⅓ c. orange juice concentrate
1 container (6 oz.) lowfat banana yogurt

Mix all fruit and set aside. Combine dry pudding with milk, orange juice, and banana yogurt; beat with wire whisk until smooth. Combine fruit and sauce. Chill. Serve garnished with fruit.

Nutrition Analysis Per Serving:

Calories 146

Protein 3g

Carbohydrate 35g

Fat <1g

(Saturated <1g)

Cholesterol 2mg

Fiber 2g

Sodium 45mg

Leaving the skin on sliced apples is tasty way to increase your fiber intake.

Strawberry-Spinach Salad

This salad makes an attractive addition to any meal, and it's bursting with flavor.

1 pint strawberries, hulled and quartered
10 oz. fresh spinach, washed,
trimmed, and torn*

Dressing:
⅓ c. sugar
¼ c. cider vinegar
2 T. canola oil
1 T. poppy seeds
¼ tsp. paprika
¼ tsp. Worcestershire sauce

For the dressing, combine the sugar, vinegar, and canola oil in a saucepan. Cook over low heat until the sugar dissolves, stirring frequently. Cool slightly. Stir in the poppy seeds, paprika, and Worcestershire sauce. For the salad, mix the strawberries and spinach in a salad bowl. Add the dressing, tossing gently to coat. Serve immediately.

To remove grit from fresh spinach and assorted greens, rinse in a mixture of 6–8 quarts water and 2 tablespoons vinegar. Rinse again in fresh water.

Yield:
6 servings

Serving Size:
⅙ of salad

Preparation Time:
10 minutes

Cooking Time:
5 minutes

Nutrition Analysis Per Serving:

Calories 114

Protein 2g

Carbohydrate 17g

Fat 5g

(Saturated <1g)

Cholesterol 0mg

Fiber 2g

Sodium 30mg

Herbed Merlot Dressing

Yield:
4 servings

Serving Size:
2 tablespoons

Preparation Time:
5 minutes

¼ c. Merlot or Cabernet Sauvignon
1 T. olive oil
1 T. chopped fresh basil
1 T. chopped fresh oregano
1 tsp. minced fresh garlic

Whisk all of the ingredients until mixed. Try this over mixed greens with toasted pine nuts and crumbles of Gorgonzola cheese.

Tip: You may substitute 1 teaspoon dried basil for the fresh basil and 1 teaspoon dried oregano leaves for the fresh oregano.

Nutrition Analysis Per Serving:

Calories 45

Protein <1g

Carbohydrate 1g

Fat 4g

(Saturated <1g)

Cholesterol 0mg

Fiber <1g

Sodium 1mg

Even though packaged salad greens are packed fresh, they can still become dehydrated with refrigeration. Place the greens in a colander and rinse them with cold water to refresh the leaves. Gently pat the leaves dry with paper towels, or use a salad spinner to remove excess moisture, before serving.

Dijon Dressing

2 T. chicken broth
2 T. white wine vinegar
1 clove garlic, minced
1 T. olive oil
1 tsp. Dijon mustard
1 tsp. Worcestershire sauce
½ tsp. sugar
¼ tsp. black pepper

Whisk all ingredients in a bowl until
the sugar dissolves. Try this over mixed
greens with toasted pecans, sliced
pears, and crumbled bleu cheese.

Yield:
4 servings

Serving Size:
2 tablespoons

Preparation Time:
5 minutes

**Nutrition Analysis
Per Serving:**

Calories 39

Protein <1g

Carbohydrate 2g

Fat 3g

(*Saturated <1g*)

Cholesterol 0mg

Fiber <1g

Sodium 56mg

Garlicky Caesar Dressing

Yield:
4 servings

Serving Size:
2 tablespoons

Preparation Time:
5 minutes

3 T. white wine vinegar
2 T. freshly grated Parmesan cheese
1 ½ T. olive oil
1 T. minced onion
3 cloves garlic, minced
2 tsp. capers
1 tsp. Dijon mustard
Salt and black pepper to taste

Combine all ingredients in a blender and process until smooth.

Nutrition Analysis Per Serving:

Calories 69

Protein 2g

Carbohydrate 2g

Fat 6g

(Saturated 1g)

Cholesterol 3mg

Fiber <1g

Sodium 136mg

Creamy Tofu Dressing

Tofu gives this reduced-fat dressing a rich, creamy texture.

¼ c. silken tofu
1 T. cider vinegar
1 tsp. honey
1 clove garlic, minced
¼ tsp. Dijon mustard
¼ tsp. celery salt
Black pepper to taste

Combine all ingredients in a blender or
food processor and process until smooth.

Yield:
4 servings

Serving Size:
2 tablespoons

Preparation Time:
5 minutes

*Use silken tofu for dressings, dips, pie fillings,
custards, or cheesecakes. It can also be
used instead of cream in Alfredo sauce or
in place of mayonnaise or sour cream.*

**Nutrition Analysis
Per Serving:**

Calories 17

Protein 1g

Carbohydrate 2g

Fat 1g

(*Saturated* <1g)

Cholesterol 0mg

Fiber <1g

Sodium 71mg

Asparagus Salmon Salad

An attractive salad that's ready in minutes.

Yield:
2 servings

Serving Size:
1 salad

Preparation Time:
20 minutes

Cooking Time:
3–5 minutes

1 T. olive oil
½ c. rice vinegar
1 tsp. Dijon mustard
¼ tsp. dried whole thyme
¼ tsp. salt
¾ lb. fresh or frozen whole asparagus
Lettuce leaves
1 can (6 ¾ oz.) salmon, drained and flaked
2 tomatoes, cut in wedges
Freshly ground pepper

Combine oil, vinegar, mustard, thyme, and salt in a jar; shake vigorously. Chill. Steam asparagus until tender (about 3–5 minutes); cool. Line salad plates with lettuce leaves. Arrange asparagus spears, salmon, and tomato wedges on lettuce. Drizzle dressing over top, season with pepper, and serve.

Nutrition Analysis Per Serving:

Calories 297

Protein 23g

Carbohydrate 21g

Fat 14g

(Saturated 2g)

Cholesterol 59mg

Fiber 6g

Sodium 758mg

Dilled Shrimp & Rice Salad

This light salad is perfect for a relaxing summer evening.

1 c. white rice, uncooked
¼ c. white wine vinegar
2 T. canola oil
1 T. chopped fresh dill, or
2 tsp. dried dillweed
½ tsp. salt
¼ tsp. black pepper
8 oz. snow peas
8 oz. medium shrimp, steamed,
peeled, and deveined
¼ c. chopped green onions
Juice of ½ lemon

Cook the rice according to package directions.
Combine the wine vinegar, canola oil, dill,
salt, and pepper in a jar with a tight-fitting
lid and shake to mix. Pour 2 tablespoons
of the dressing over the hot rice in a bowl
and toss gently. Cover and chill for 1 hour
or longer. Steam the snow peas in a steamer
until tender; drain. Combine the rice, shrimp,
green onions, and remaining dressing in a bowl
and mix well. Mound the rice mixture on a
large serving platter or on individual dinner
plates. Arrange the snow peas spoke-fashion
around the outer edge of the rice. Drizzle with
lemon juice just before serving. Garnish with
additional dill and/or additional green onions.

Yield:
4 servings

Serving Size:
1 ½ cups

Preparation Time:
20–25 minutes

Chilling Time:
1 hour

Cooking Time:
35 minutes

**Nutrition Analysis
Per Serving:**

Calories 312

Protein 13g

Carbohydrate 46g

Fat 8g

(Saturated 1g)

Cholesterol 67mg

Fiber 2g

Sodium 374mg

Spinach Salad with Chicken

Spinach salad lovers—this salad's for you!

Yield:
4 servings

Serving Size:
1 ½ cups

Preparation Time:
35 minutes

Chilling Time:
30 minutes

**Nutrition Analysis
Per Serving:**

Calories 313

Protein 27g

Carbohydrate 28g

Fat 13g

(Saturated 2g)

Cholesterol 45mg

Fiber 12g

Sodium 580mg

Dressing:
⅓ c. cider vinegar
3 T. water
1 T. canola oil
2 T. brown sugar
2 T. chopped green onion
2 tsp. Dijon mustard
½ tsp. salt
¼ tsp. black pepper

Salad:
3 bunches fresh spinach, washed and torn
1 ½ c. cooked chicken, cubed and chilled
½ lb. mushrooms, sliced
1 small avocado, peeled and sliced
¼ c. chopped green onion
1 can (8 oz.) sliced water chestnuts, drained
1 ½ c. alfalfa sprouts (optional)

Combine dressing ingredients in a jar; shake vigorously. Chill at least 30 minutes. Toss together spinach, chicken, mushrooms, avocado, green onion, and water chestnuts. Serve drizzled with dressing and topped with sprouts, if desired.

Oriental Chicken Salad

This is a salad that packs a lot of crunch, and flavor.

Dressing:
¾ c. white wine vinegar
¼ c. sugar
1 tsp. sesame oil
1 tsp. canola oil
½ tsp. salt
¼ tsp. black pepper

Salad:
3 c. (about 1 lb.) cubed cooked chicken
1 large head Romaine lettuce, shredded
⅓ c. diced celery
3 green onions, chopped
1 can (11 oz.) mandarin oranges, drained
1 c. chow mein noodles

Combine vinegar, sugar, oils, salt, and pepper in a small saucepan. Heat until sugar is dissolved, stirring frequently. Set aside to cool. Toss chicken, lettuce, celery, and onion together; mix with cooled dressing. Top with mandarin oranges and chow mein noodles.

Salad greens will keep up to two weeks if stored properly in the refrigerator. Before refrigerating, wash lettuce and let drain; while still damp, roll the lettuce up in paper towels and place it in a plastic bag. Fresh herbs also keep longer when stored in this manner.

Yield:
6 servings

Serving Size:
1 ½ cups

Preparation Time:
10 minutes

Cooking Time:
10 minutes

Nutrition Analysis Per Serving:

Calories 254

Protein 24g

Carbohydrate 24g

Fat 6g

(Saturated 1g)

Cholesterol 60mg

Fiber 2g

Sodium 301mg

Polynesian Chicken Salad

A mountain café in Aspen inspired this recipe. We know you'll agree it's simply the best.

Yield:
4 servings

Serving Size:
¾ cup

Preparation Time:
10 minutes

2 c. (8 oz.) diced cooked chicken breast
¾ c. pineapple chunks, drained
½ c. diced celery
¼ c. slivered almonds, toasted
4 green onions, chopped
½ c. plain nonfat or lowfat yogurt
¼ c. light mayonnaise
Romaine lettuce leaves

Combine chicken, pineapple, celery, almonds, and onions; set aside. Blend together yogurt and mayonnaise; stir into chicken mixture. Serve on a bed of lettuce.

Nutrition Analysis Per Serving:

Calories 251

Protein 25g

Carbohydrate 13g

Fat 11g

(Saturated 2g)

Cholesterol 65mg

Fiber 2g

Sodium 203mg

Raspberry Grilled Chicken Salad

This colorful salad celebrates summer's berry harvest, and makes a light meal when served with fresh sourdough or French bread.

4 boneless, skinless chicken breast halves
⅓ c. raspberry preserves
⅓ c. frozen orange juice concentrate
½ c. reduced-sodium soy sauce
2 T. rice vinegar
½ tsp. chili powder
½ tsp. garlic powder
6 c. mixed salad greens
⅓ c. fat-free or light raspberry vinaigrette
½ c. fresh raspberries

Place the chicken in a sealable plastic bag. Combine the preserves, orange juice concentrate, soy sauce, rice vinegar, chili powder, and garlic powder in a bowl and mix well. Pour over the chicken and seal tightly. Toss to coat. Marinate in the refrigerator for 2 hours or longer, turning occasionally. Grill the chicken over hot coals for 5–6 minutes per side or until cooked through. Cut into ½-inch strips. Toss the salad greens with the vinaigrette in a bowl. Arrange an equal amount of the salad greens on each plate. Top with the chicken. Sprinkle with the raspberries.

Yield:
4 servings

Preparation Time:
15 minutes

Marinating Time:
2 hours

Cooking Time:
12 minutes

Nutrition Analysis Per Serving:

Calories 457

Protein 57g

Carbohydrate 39g

Fat 7g

(Saturated 2g)

Cholesterol 146mg

Fiber 3g

Sodium 862mg

Steak & Roasted Vegetable Salad

Yield:
4 servings

Serving Size:
1 salad

Preparation Time:
30 minutes

Cooking Time:
50 minutes

Nutrition Analysis Per Serving:

Calories 274

Protein 31g

Carbohydrate 23g

Fat 7g

(*Saturated 2g*)

Cholesterol 75mg

Fiber 7g

Sodium 655mg

Cooking spray
1 medium zucchini, cut into 1-inch slices
1 medium eggplant, cut into 1-inch slices
1 large red or green bell pepper,
cut into 1-inch strips
1 medium onion, cut into 1-inch wedges
16 small mushrooms
¾ c. fat-free or lowfat Italian salad dressing
2 T. balsamic vinegar
2 cloves garlic, crushed
1 tsp. crushed dried rosemary
¼ tsp. black pepper and salt, to taste
1 lb. (1-inch thick) beef top loin
8 cups torn lettuce

Spray a 10 x 15-inch pan lightly with non-stick cooking spray. Arrange the zucchini, eggplant, red pepper, onion, and mushrooms in the pan. Spray vegetables generously with non-stick cooking spray. Whisk the salad dressing, balsamic vinegar, garlic, rosemary, and pepper in a bowl. Drizzle over the vegetables. Roast at 425° for 30–35 minutes or until vegetables are tender, stirring once.

Heat a large non-stick skillet over medium heat. Add the beef. Cook for 12–15 minutes for medium-rare to medium, turning once. Let stand for 10 minutes. Sprinkle with the salt. Trim the fat from the beef. Slice against the grain into thin strips. Arrange equal amounts of the lettuce on each plate. Arrange the beef and roasted vegetables over the lettuce. Serve immediately.

Spicy Pork Tenderloin Salad

Enjoy this colorful salad, then lean back and let the cool mountain air lull you to sleep.

2 c. fresh spinach, torn
½ c. chopped green onions
12 cherry tomatoes, halved
1 can (12 oz.) whole kernel corn, drained
½ tsp. chili powder
¼ tsp. cumin
¼ tsp. garlic powder
1 lb. pork tenderloin, cut into ¼-inch slices
1 T. olive oil
½ c. orange juice
2 T. lime juice

Yield:
4 servings

Serving Size:
1 salad

Preparation Time:
20 minutes

Cooking Time:
20 minutes

In a large bowl, combine spinach, onion, tomatoes, and corn; set aside. In a medium bowl, combine chili powder, cumin, and garlic powder. Add pork and toss to coat. In a non-stick skillet, heat oil over high heat. Sauté pork until golden brown; stir in orange and lime juices. Spoon pork mixture over vegetables; toss gently to coat.

Nutrition Analysis Per Serving:

Calories 259

Protein 27g

Carbohydrate 19g

Fat 8g

(Saturated 2g)

Cholesterol 74mg

Fiber 4g

Sodium 353mg

Quick Taco Salad

Keep these ingredients on hand to make a light Mexican dinner at the end of a busy day.

Yield:
4 servings

Serving Size:
1 salad

Preparation Time:
10 minutes

Cooking Time:
5 minutes

1 can (15 oz.) beans with tomatoes, peppers, and Mexican spices
6 c. shredded lettuce
½ c. (2 oz.) shredded, reduced-fat sharp Cheddar cheese
1 small avocado, peeled and sliced
1 large tomato, chopped
4 oz. baked tortilla chips

Place beans in a saucepan and heat thoroughly. On a serving plate, layer lettuce, beans, cheese, avocado, and tomato. Arrange tortilla chips around edge; serve with your favorite prepared salsa.

Nutrition Analysis Per Serving:

Calories 375

Protein 14g

Carbohydrate 53g

Fat 17g

(Saturated 3g)

Cholesterol 10mg

Fiber 12g

Sodium 706mg

Vegetables

Awesome Asparagus

An easy way to dress up asparagus.

Yield:
4 servings

Serving Size:
¼ lb. asparagus

Preparation Time:
5 minutes

Cooking Time:
5–10 minutes

1 lb. fresh asparagus, trimmed
1 ½ T. butter, melted
2 tsp. balsamic vinegar
1 T. pine nuts or other chopped nuts, toasted

Steam the asparagus in a steamer until tender-crisp; drain. Arrange on a serving platter. Whisk the butter and balsamic vinegar in a bowl. Drizzle over the asparagus. Sprinkle with pine nuts.

Nutrition Analysis Per Serving:

Calories 78

Protein 3g

Carbohydrate 6g

Fat 6g

(Saturated 3g)

Cholesterol 12mg

Fiber 2g

Sodium 47mg

Balsamic vinegar, once an obscure condiment in Italy, has now become a popular ingredient in reduced-fat recipes. Balsamic vinegar is less acidic than most vinegars and adds a gentle sweetness to any dish.

Sweet & Sour Carrots

1 lb. carrots, diagonally sliced
1 medium green bell pepper, diced
1 can (8 oz.) pineapple chunks (in own juice)
⅓ c. sugar
1 T. cornstarch
½ tsp. salt
2 T. cider vinegar
2 tsp. low-sodium soy sauce

Steam the carrots in a steamer for 4–6 minutes or until tender-crisp; drain. Add green pepper and cook 3 minutes longer; drain and set aside. Drain pineapple juice into measuring cup; add water to measure ⅓ cup liquid. Reserve pineapple chunks.

In a small saucepan, combine sugar, cornstarch, and salt. Stir in pineapple liquid, vinegar, and soy sauce until smooth. Stirring over medium heat, bring to a boil and simmer 1–2 minutes until thickened. Pour over carrots and green pepper; stir in pineapple. Serve hot or cold.

One of the benefits of eating carrots is that they contain carotene. In your body, carotene is converted into vitamin A and may protect against some diseases such as cancer.

Yield:
6 servings

Serving Size:
½ cup

Preparation Time:
15 minutes

Cooking Time:
12 minutes

Nutrition Analysis Per Serving:

Calories 106

Protein 1g

Carbohydrate 26g

Fat <1g

(Saturated <1g)

Cholesterol 0mg

Fiber 3g

Sodium 309mg

Maple-Glazed Carrots

Yield:
6 servings

Serving Size:
½ cup

Preparation Time:
10 minutes

Cooking Time:
10 minutes

1 lb. baby carrots, julienne cut
1 T. lemon juice
1 T. maple syrup
1 tsp. butter
⅛ tsp. cinnamon
Salt and black pepper, to taste

Steam the carrots in a steamer for 4–6 minutes or until tender-crisp; drain. Cover to keep warm. Combine the lemon juice, maple syrup, butter, cinnamon, salt, and pepper in a saucepan. Cook just until the butter melts, stirring occasionally. Add the carrots, tossing to coat. Serve immediately.

Nutrition Analysis Per Serving:

Calories 44

Protein 1g

Carbohydrate 9g

Fat 1g

(Saturated <1g)

Cholesterol 2mg

Fiber 1g

Sodium 33mg

Steam or microwave vegetables in as little water as possible. Both vitamins and minerals can seep into the cooking water and be lost when drained. If you have to use a considerable amount of water, as when boiling potatoes, save the cooking water to make soups or sauces in the future.

Green Beans Telluride

Serve with Smoky Beef Brisket (p. 215) and hot whole-wheat rolls.

**2 cans (16 oz. each) uncut
green beans, undrained
1 can (8 oz.) sliced water chestnuts, drained
Cooking spray
¼ c. chopped green onion
½ c. lowfat sour cream
1 tsp. sugar
1 tsp. vinegar
Salt and black pepper, to taste**

Heat beans in a saucepan. Add chestnuts
and continue to heat 2 minutes. Meanwhile,
in a small saucepan coated with cooking
spray, sauté onions until tender. Stir
remaining ingredients into onions and warm
over medium heat—don't boil. To serve,
drain bean mixture and toss with sauce.

Yield:
6 servings

Serving Size:
½ cup

Preparation Time:
5 minutes

Cooking Time:
10 minutes

**Nutrition Analysis
Per Serving:**

Calories 82

Protein 3g

Carbohydrate 13g

Fat 2g

(*Saturated 1g*)

Cholesterol 7mg

Fiber 5g

Sodium 438mg

Vail Vegetable Medley

Yield:
8 servings

Serving Size:
½ cup

Preparation Time:
10 minutes

Cooking Time:
7 minutes

1 large sweet red bell pepper
1 large sweet yellow pepper
2 large carrots, cut into strips
1 medium onion, diced
2 cloves garlic, minced
1 tsp. olive oil
2 large zucchini, julienne cut
2 tsp. dried whole basil
½ tsp. salt
½ tsp. pepper

Seed red and yellow pepper and cut into ¼-inch strips. Sauté peppers, carrots, onion, and garlic in oil in a non-stick skillet for 5 minutes. Add zucchini strips and cook for 2 minutes or until vegetables are tender. Stir in basil, salt, and pepper.

Nutrition Analysis Per Serving:

Calories 47

Protein 2g

Carbohydrate 9g

Fat 1g

(Saturated <1g)

Cholesterol 0mg

Fiber 3g

Sodium 168mg

Red peppers have nearly four times as much vitamin C as oranges.

Fire-Grilled Vegetables

1 large green bell pepper,
seeded and quartered
1 large red bell pepper, seeded and quartered
1 medium yellow squash,
cut into ¼-inch slices
1 medium zucchini, cut into ¼-inch slices
¼ c. lowfat Italian dressing
1 T. balsamic vinegar
1 T. chopped fresh basil, or 1 tsp. dried basil

Combine the peppers, yellow squash, and
zucchini in a bowl and mix gently. Whisk the
Italian dressing, balsamic vinegar, and basil
in a bowl. Pour over the vegetables, tossing
to coat. Grill the vegetables over medium-
hot coals for 10–12 minutes or until the
desired degree of crispness, turning once.

*For an economical and convenient way to
enjoy flavorful bell peppers, buy them in large
quantities when they are on sale. Wash, seed,
and slice or chop them; then spread them on a
baking sheet sprayed lightly with vegetable oil.
Freeze them until firm. Transfer the peppers to
freezer bags, and store them up to three months.*

Yield:
6 servings

Serving Size:
½ cup

Preparation Time:
15 minutes

Cooking Time:
10–12 minutes

**Nutrition Analysis
Per Serving:**

Calories 31

Protein 1g

Carbohydrate 7g

Fat <1g

(Saturated <1g)

Cholesterol 0mg

Fiber 2g

Sodium 169mg

Grilled Peppers & Potatoes

A unique complement to grilled meat that provides a pleasant alternative to traditional potato salad.

Yield:
4 servings

Serving Size:
1 cup

Preparation Time:
10–15 minutes

Cooking Time:
45 minutes

1 lb. new potatoes, quartered
1 medium sweet red or green
bell pepper, cubed
1 medium onion, sliced
1 T. olive oil
1 ½ tsp. dried rosemary
1 clove garlic, minced
⅛ tsp. crushed red pepper flakes (optional)
½ tsp. salt

Combine potatoes, pepper, and onion in a large bowl; set aside. Heat oil, rosemary, garlic, and pepper flakes together in a small saucepan. Remove from heat. Toss olive oil mixture with vegetables; sprinkle with salt. Place vegetables in a large square of heavy-duty aluminum foil; seal. Place foil package on grill over medium to hot coals. Cook for 45 minutes, turning once.

Nutrition Analysis Per Serving:

Calories 128

Protein 3g

Carbohydrate 20g

Fat 4g

(Saturated Fat 1g)

Cholesterol 0mg

Fiber 3g

Sodium 296mg

"Light" olive oil isn't any lower in calories or fat than regular olive oil. It's just milder in flavor.

Roaring Fork Ratatouille

Cooking spray
1 medium onion, diced
4 cloves garlic, crushed
1 small eggplant, peeled and cubed
2 medium green bell peppers,
sliced into strips
1 c. tomato juice
3 T. dry red wine
1 bay leaf
1 tsp. dried basil
1 tsp. dried marjoram
½ tsp. dried oregano leaves
1 tsp. salt
1 medium zucchini, sliced
2 medium tomatoes, diced
½ c. water (if needed)

Yield:
6 servings

Serving Size:
1 cup

Preparation Time:
20 minutes

Cooking Time:
30 minutes

Lightly coat a large pot with cooking spray.
Add onion and garlic; sauté until tender (about
5 minutes). Add eggplant, peppers, tomato
juice, wine, and seasonings; mix well. Cover and
simmer until vegetables are tender (about 10–15
minutes). Add zucchini and tomatoes, cover and
simmer 10 more minutes or until all vegetables
are tender. (Add water as needed.) Serve as
a hearty vegetable stew or on a bed of rice.

*Preventing moisture loss in vegetables is
important in maintaining quality and freshness.
Some food companies coat vegetables with
a harmless wax to prevent such losses.*

**Nutrition Analysis
Per Serving:**

Calories 66

Protein 3g

Carbohydrate 14g

Fat <1g

(Saturated <1g)

Cholesterol 0mg

Fiber 2g

Sodium 478mg

Sesame Broccoli

Yield:
6 servings

Serving Size:
⅔ cup

Preparation Time:
5 minutes

Cooking Time:
6–10 minutes

4 c. broccoli florets
2 T. rice vinegar
1 T. water
½ tsp. sesame oil
1 tsp. lemon juice
½ tsp. ground ginger
1 tsp. sesame seeds, toasted

Arrange broccoli in a vegetable steamer over boiling water. Cover and steam 6–8 minutes or until tender. Place in a serving dish; set aside and keep warm. Combine vinegar, water, oil, lemon juice, and ginger; pour over broccoli and toss to coat. Sprinkle with sesame seeds.

Nutrition Analysis Per Serving:

Calories 26

Protein 1g

Carbohydrate 4g

Fat 1g

(Saturated <1g)

Cholesterol 0mg

Fiber 1g

Sodium 16mg

Rice vinegar is a sweet, mild vinegar that makes an excellent dressing combined with seasonings or all by itself.

Broccoli with Dill Cheese Sauce

4 c. broccoli florets
½ c. water

Cheese Sauce:
1 c. lowfat buttermilk
¼ c. grated Parmesan cheese
1 tsp. Dijon mustard
2 tsp. cornstarch
1 tsp. dried dillweed

Place broccoli florets and water in a microwave-safe dish. Cover dish with plastic wrap and microwave on high power for 8–10 minutes or until tender. Meanwhile, combine buttermilk, Parmesan cheese, Dijon mustard, and cornstarch in a small saucepan over medium-low heat. Using a wire whisk, stir constantly until sauce boils. Continue to cook over low heat for 2 more minutes. Stir in dill and serve over drained broccoli.

Microwaving vegetables is quick and convenient, and it helps retain the flavor and many of the nutrients found in the vegetables.

Yield:
4 servings

Serving Size:
1 cup

Preparation Time:
8 minutes

Cooking Time:
2–5 minutes

Nutrition Analysis Per Serving:

Calories 77

Protein 6g

Carbohydrate 9g

Fat 2g

(*Saturated 1g*)

Cholesterol 7mg

Fiber 2g

Sodium 195mg

Broccoli Dijon

Yield:
4 servings

Serving Size:
½ cup

Preparation Time:
5 minutes

Cooking Time:
10 minutes

1 T. Dijon mustard
1 T. low-sodium soy sauce
1 T. white wine vinegar
1 tsp. canola oil, or other vegetable oil
2 c. broccoli florets

Whisk the Dijon mustard, soy sauce, wine vinegar, and canola oil in a bowl. Steam the broccoli in a steamer until tender-crisp; drain. Arrange the broccoli on a serving platter. Drizzle with mustard mixture. Serve immediately.

Nutrition Analysis Per Serving:

Calories 30

Protein 2g

Carbohydrate 3g

Fat 2g

(Saturated <1g)

Cholesterol 0mg

Fiber 1g

Sodium 231mg

Grilled Corn-on-the-Cob

4 ears fresh corn
Butter-flavored cooking spray
½ tsp. lemon-pepper seasoning

Remove husks and silks from corn just before grilling. Coat each ear with cooking spray and sprinkle with lemon-pepper seasoning. Place each ear on a piece of heavy-duty aluminum foil and roll up; twist foil at each end. Grill, covered, over medium-hot coals for 20 minutes, turning occasionally.

Yield:
4 servings

Serving Size:
1 ear

Preparation Time:
5 minutes

Cooking Time:
20 minutes

Nutrition Analysis Per Serving:

Calories 122

Protein 5g

Carbohydrate 27g

Fat 2g

(Saturated <1g)

Cholesterol 0mg

Fiber 5g

Sodium 36mg

Eat fresh corn as soon as possible for the best sweet flavor. A chemical reaction converts the sugar in corn into starch after it is picked. For this reason, old corn won't be as sweet and delicious.

Skillet Zucchini Pancake

A great recipe for a bumper zucchini crop!

Yield:
4 servings

Serving Size:
¼ of pancake

Preparation Time:
15 minutes

Cooking Time
14–18 minutes

**Nutrition Analysis
Per Serving:**

Calories 99

Protein 6g

Carbohydrate 11g

Fat 4g

(Saturated 1g)

Cholesterol 54mg

Fiber 2g

Sodium 96mg

2 c. grated zucchini (squeezed dry)
¾ c. peeled, grated potato (squeezed dry)
¼ c. chopped green onion
2 T. flour
1 whole egg, beaten
2 egg whites
1 clove garlic, crushed
Salt and black pepper, to taste
2 tsp. margarine, divided
1 T. grated Parmesan cheese

In a medium bowl, combine zucchini, potato, green onion, flour, egg, egg whites, garlic, salt, and pepper. Melt 1 teaspoon margarine in a non-stick skillet over moderate heat, making sure bottom and sides of pan are well coated. Add zucchini mixture, shaping it into a cake with a spatula; cook uncovered over medium heat until golden around the edges (8–10 minutes). Place a large plate over the skillet and invert the pancake onto it. Add the remaining margarine to the skillet; melt over moderate heat. Slide the pancake back into the skillet and cook uncovered until firm (about 6–8 minutes). Sprinkle with Parmesan cheese.

Green Chile Squash

1 medium onion, chopped
1 T. canola oil
5 c. zucchini, sliced
1 pkg. (16 oz.) frozen corn
1 can (4 oz.) chopped green chiles
¼ c. water
Salt, to taste

In a large nonstick skillet, sauté onion in oil. When onions are soft, add zucchini, corn, green chiles, water, and salt. Cover and cook over low heat 10–15 minutes, or until zucchini is tender.

Fill half of your plate with vegetables to create a meal with more eye appeal and fewer calories.

Yield:
8 servings

Serving Size:
⅔ cup

Preparation Time:
5 minutes

Cooking Time:
15–20 minutes

Nutrition Analysis Per Serving:

Calories 87

Protein 3g

Carbohydrate 16g

Fat 2g

(Saturated <1g)

Cholesterol 0mg

Fiber 3g

Sodium 62mg

Spaghetti Squash Marinara

A truly fun vegetable!

Yield:
6 servings

Serving Size:
1 cup

Preparation Time:
5 minutes

Cooking Time:
10 minutes

**1 medium spaghetti squash
(about 3–3 ½ lbs.)
3 c. your favorite marinara sauce
¼ c. grated Parmesan cheese**

Cut spaghetti squash in half length-wise and remove seeds. Place squash halves, cut side down, in a large glass baking dish. Add 3 tablespoons water. Cover dish with plastic wrap and microwave on high for 8–10 minutes or until tender. Drain squash. Using a fork, remove spaghetti-like strands of squash by scraping gently across the tender "pulp" inside each half. Warm marinara sauce over medium heat. Portion spaghetti squash on plates, top with sauce, then sprinkle evenly with cheese.

**Nutrition Analysis
Per Serving:**

Calories 156

Protein 5g

Carbohydrate 26g

Fat 5g

(Saturated 1g)

Cholesterol 3mg

Fiber 4g

Sodium 605mg

Spaghetti squash is a yellow, football-shaped vegetable with pale yellow, stringy meat that resembles spaghetti when it is cooked and teased apart with a fork.

Rosemary Potatoes

A great side dish that can be cooked in foil packets over an open campfire.

2 green onions, finely chopped
1 T. olive oil
1 tsp. crushed dried rosemary
½ tsp. garlic salt
2 lbs. unpeeled red potatoes,
cut into ½-inch cubes

Preheat oven to 400°. Combine the green onions, olive oil, rosemary, and garlic salt in a bowl. Add the red potatoes, tossing to coat. Spread the potatoes in a 9 x 13-inch baking pan. Bake, covered with foil, for 25–30 minutes or until brown and tender.

Keep the skin intact on fruits and vegetables as much as possible. Peeling removes nutrients concentrated just under the skin and takes away valuable fiber.

Yield:
6 servings

Serving Size:
½ cup

Preparation Time:
15 minutes

Cooking Time:
25–30 minutes

Nutrition Analysis Per Serving:

Calories 155

Protein 3g

Carbohydrate 31g

Fat 2g

(Saturated <1g)

Cholesterol 0mg

Fiber 3g

Sodium 161mg

Garlic Mashers

This light version of garlic mashed potatoes is so flavorful you will never miss the gravy.

Yield:
6 servings

Serving Size:
½ cup

Preparation Time:
20 minutes

Cooking Time:
30 minutes

1 ½ lbs. unpeeled red potatoes, cut into 1-inch cubes
2 T. butter
1 T. minced garlic
½ c. skim milk
1 tsp. prepared horseradish
Salt and black pepper, to taste

Combine the red potatoes with enough water to cover in a saucepan. Bring to a boil; reduce heat. Simmer for 30 minutes or until tender; drain. Heat the butter in a saucepan over medium heat until melted. Add the garlic and sauté until light brown; stir in the skim milk. Cook over low heat just until warm, stirring constantly. Stir in the horseradish and remove from heat.

Beat the potatoes in a mixer bowl just until mashed. Add the milk mixture and beat until blended. Season with salt and pepper. The potatoes should be slightly lumpy.

Nutrition Analysis Per Serving:

Calories 146

Protein 3g

Carbohydrate 25g

Fat 4g

(*Saturated 2g*)

Cholesterol 11mg

Fiber 2g

Sodium 60mg

Tangy Mashed Potatoes

2 lbs. potatoes, peeled and cubed
1 c. plain nonfat or lowfat yogurt
¼ c. chopped green onions
1 T. margarine
Salt and black pepper, to taste

Place potatoes in boiling water and cook until tender (about 20 minutes); drain.
In a bowl, combine potatoes, yogurt, and margarine. Beat with an electric mixer until fluffy. Stir in green onion; season with salt and black pepper to taste. Serve hot.

Yield:
6 servings

Serving Size:
⅔ cup

Preparation Time:
10 minutes

Cooking Time:
20 minutes

Nutrition Analysis Per Serving:

Calories 155

Protein 5g

Carbohydrate 31g

Fat 2g

(Saturated <1g)

Cholesterol 1mg

Fiber 2g

Sodium 53mg

Bananas are often recommended as a high potassium food, but potatoes actually contain twice as much potassium.

Oven Fries

Oh-so-satisfying when the urge for French fries hits!

Yield:
8 servings

Serving Size:
4 wedges

Preparation Time:
5–10 minutes

Cooking Time:
45–60 minutes

2 tsp. grated Parmesan cheese
1 tsp. salt
1 tsp. sugar
½ tsp. garlic powder
½ tsp. paprika
¼ tsp. onion powder
¼ tsp. chili powder
¼ tsp. lemon-pepper seasoning
4 large potatoes
1 T. olive oil
1 T. water

Preheat oven to 350°. Mix cheese and seasonings. Cut each potato into 8 wedges. Combine oil and water. Brush wedges with oil and water mixture and place on baking sheet. Sprinkle potatoes with seasoning mixture. Bake until soft when pricked with a fork, about 45 minutes. For crisp fries, bake 1 hour.

Nutrition Analysis Per Serving:

Calories 102

Protein 2g

Carbohydrate 19g

Fat 2g

(Saturated <1g)

Cholesterol <1mg

Fiber 2g

Sodium 308mg

Monounsaturated fats such as canola oil and olive oil can help lower blood cholesterol levels. However, they still contain the same number of calories as any other oil.

Praline Sweet Potatoes

1 can (16 oz.) sweet potatoes, drained
1 egg, beaten
2 T. sugar
¼ tsp. vanilla extract
⅓ c. packed dark brown sugar
2 T. chopped pecans
2 T. flour
2 tsp. margarine, melted

Mash the sweet potatoes in a bowl. Stir in the egg, sugar, and vanilla. Spoon into a greased 2-quart shallow baking dish. Combine the brown sugar, pecans, flour, and margarine in a bowl and mix well. Add more flour if the mixture is not crumbly. Sprinkle over the sweet potato mixture. Bake at 350° for 25–30 minutes or until light brown. Cover with foil as soon as the sweet potatoes begin to bubble to prevent the pecans from burning.

Tip: You may substitute 1 pound fresh sweet potatoes, baked and then mashed, for the canned sweet potatoes.

Yield:
4 servings

Serving Size:
½ cup

Preparation Time:
15 minutes

Cooking Time:
25–30 minutes

Nutrition Analysis Per Serving:

Calories 271

Protein 4g

Carbohydrate 52g

Fat 6g

(Saturated 1g)

Cholesterol 53mg

Fiber 2g

Sodium 105mg

Sweet Potatoes with Tart Cherries

This delicious sweet potato dish was adapted from a recipe served at Washington Park Grille, in Denver.

Yield:
8 servings

Serving Size:
½ cup

Preparation Time:
20–25 minutes

Cooking Time:
30–40 minutes

Nutrition Analysis Per Serving:

Calories 161

Protein 2g

Carbohydrate 37g

Fat 2g

(Saturated <1g)

Cholesterol 0mg

Fiber 3g

Sodium 6mg

½ c. dried sour cherries
1 c. hot water
3 medium sweet potatoes, peeled and cut into ½-inch cubes
2 pears, peeled and cut into ½-inch cubes
2 Granny Smith apples, peeled and cut into ½-inch cubes
3 T. honey
1 T. olive oil
¾ tsp. cinnamon
½ tsp. nutmeg
Salt and black pepper, to taste

Preheat oven to 400°. Place cherries in a small bowl. Pour enough hot water over the cherries to cover. Let stand for 2 minutes; drain. Combine the cherries, sweet potatoes, pears, and apples in a large bowl and mix well. Spoon cherry mixture into a 9 x 13 x 2-inch pan. Combine the honey, olive oil, cinnamon, nutmeg, salt, and pepper in a microwave-safe bowl and mix well. Microwave on medium for 30 seconds and stir. Pour over the sweet potato mixture, stirring to coat. Bake for 30–40 minutes or until the sweet potatoes are tender.

When it comes to fruits and vegetables, think of a rainbow. Eating a variety of colorful fruit and vegetables provides you with more nutrients. Plus your meals will look beautiful!

Breads, Muffins, & Scones

Cranberry-Walnut Bread

Yield:
1 loaf

Serving Size:
1 slice

Preparation Time:
20–25 minutes

Cooking Time:
65–75 minutes

2 c. flour
¾ c. sugar
1 ½ tsp. baking powder
½ tsp. baking soda
½ tsp. salt
¾ c. orange juice
2 T. canola oil
1 egg
1 ½ c. coarsely chopped fresh cranberries
⅓ c. chopped walnuts
1 T. grated orange peel
Cooking spray

Nutrition Analysis Per Serving:

Calories 187

Protein 3g

Carbohydrate 32g

Fat 5g

(Saturated <1g)

Cholesterol 18mg

Fiber 2g

Sodium 217mg

Preheat oven to 350°. In a large bowl, combine flour, sugar, baking powder, baking soda, and salt. In a medium bowl, beat together orange juice, oil, and egg until blended. Stir juice mixture into flour mixture just until moistened. Gently stir in cranberries, walnuts, and orange peel. Spoon batter evenly into an 8 ½ x 4 ½ x 2 ½-inch loaf pan coated with cooking spray. Bake 65–75 minutes or until a wooden pick inserted into the center comes out clean. Cool bread in pan for 10 minutes, then remove from pan and cool on wire rack.

Generally, you don't need to sift all-purpose flour before measuring it since it is pre-sifted. On the other hand, cake flour should always be sifted before measuring.

Blue Ribbon Zucchini Bread

This bread freezes beautifully. Keep a loaf in the freezer for spur-of-the-moment entertaining.

3 eggs, beaten
½ c. sugar
1 c. packed brown sugar
½ c. oil
1 T. maple flavoring
2 c. shredded zucchini
2 tsp. baking soda
½ tsp. baking powder
1 tsp. salt
½ c. wheat germ
2 ½ c. flour
⅓ c. walnuts, chopped
Cooking spray

Preheat oven to 350°. Beat together eggs, sugars, oil, and maple flavoring until foamy and thick; stir in zucchini. Stir in baking soda, baking powder, salt, wheat germ, and flour; mix well. Add nuts. Spoon batter into two 9 x 5 x 3-inch loaf pans coated with cooking spray and flour. Bake 45 minutes to 1 hour, or until toothpick inserted into center comes out clean. Cool 10 minutes before removing from pans.

Resist the temptation to spread margarine or butter on bread. Fresh, flavorful quick breads like Blue Ribbon Zucchini Bread have a wonderful taste on their own.

Yield:
2 loaves

Serving Size:
1 slice

Preparation Time:
15–20 minutes

Cooking Time:
45 minutes–1 hour

Nutrition Analysis Per Serving:

Calories 181

Protein 3g

Carbohydrate 25g

Fat 8g

(Saturated 1g)

Cholesterol 26mg

Fiber 1g

Sodium 226mg

Harvest Pumpkin Bread

When autumn comes, serve this bread warm from the oven with piping hot soup.

Yield:
1 loaf

Serving Size:
1 slice

Preparation Time:
20 minutes

Cooking Time:
60–70 minutes

2 eggs, beaten
1 c. sugar
1 c. canned pumpkin
⅓ c. oil
¼ c. water
1 ⅔ c. flour
1 tsp. baking soda
¾ tsp. salt
½ tsp. baking powder
½ tsp. ground cloves
½ tsp. nutmeg
½ tsp. cinnamon
Cooking spray

Preheat oven to 350°. Combine eggs, sugar, pumpkin, oil, and water. Sift flour and remaining ingredients together and add to pumpkin mixture; stir well. Place in an 8 ½ x 4 ½ x 2 ½-inch loaf pan coated with cooking spray and flour. Bake for 60–70 minutes or until loaf sounds hollow when tapped. Allow bread to cool for 10 minutes, then remove from pan.

Nutrition Analysis Per Serving:

Calories 201

Protein 3g

Carbohydrate 32g

Fat 7g

(Saturated <1g)

Cholesterol 35mg

Fiber 1g

Sodium 284mg

Place bread in the center of a preheated oven so heat can circulate freely and evenly.

Gold Rush Carrot Bread

Truly a 24-karat bread.

½ c. orange juice
⅓ c. oil
¼ c. sugar
1 egg, beaten
2 tsp. vanilla
1 c. whole-wheat flour
1 c. flour
1 T. cinnamon
1 tsp. baking powder
½ tsp. baking soda
¼ tsp. salt
1 ¼ c. grated carrots
Cooking spray

Yield:
1 loaf

Serving Size:
1 slice

Preparation Time:
17 minutes

Cooking Time:
40–50 minutes

Preheat oven to 350°. Combine orange juice, oil, sugar, egg, and vanilla in a large mixing bowl; set aside. Combine whole-wheat flour, flour, cinnamon, baking powder, baking soda, and salt; mix well. Add dry ingredients to orange juice mixture, stirring just until dry ingredients are moistened. Fold in carrots. Bake in a 9 x 5 x 3-inch loaf pan coated with cooking spray for 40–45 minutes or until a wooden pick inserted in center comes out clean.

Baked products that use a combination of all-purpose flour and whole-wheat flour have a lighter texture than those that use only whole-wheat flour. They also have more fiber than recipes that use only all-purpose flour.

Nutrition Analysis Per Serving:

Calories 162

Protein 3g

Carbohydrate 22g

Fat 7g

(Saturated 1g)

Cholesterol 18mg

Fiber 2g

Sodium 156mg

Dude Ranch Whole-wheat Biscuits

Yield:
16 Servings

Serving Size:
1 biscuit

Preparation Time:
15 minutes

Cooking Time:
10–12 minutes

2 c. flour
¾ c. whole-wheat flour
4 tsp. baking powder
½ tsp. salt
¼ c. margarine, softened
1 c. skim milk
Cooking spray

Preheat oven to 450°. Combine first 4 ingredients; cut in margarine with a pastry blender until mixture resembles coarse meal. Add milk, stirring until dry ingredients are moistened. Turn dough onto a lightly floured surface; knead about 1 minute. Shape dough into 16 balls and place them in a 9-inch-square baking pan coated with cooking spray. Flatten dough balls slightly; bake 10–12 minutes or until lightly browned.

Nutrition Analysis Per Serving:

Calories 111

Protein 3g

Carbohydrate 18g

Fat 3g

(*Saturated 1g*)

Cholesterol <1mg

Fiber 1g

Sodium 236mg

Substituting reduced-calorie margarine for regular margarine works well in many recipes, except baked items. Because reduced-calorie margarines have water whipped into them, the result can be wetter and less flaky baked goods.

Swedish Rye Bread

¼ c. warm water (105–115°)
1 pkg. rapid-rise yeast
1 ½ c. rye flour
¼ c. molasses
¼ c. packed brown sugar
1 T. salt
1 T. caraway seeds
1 T. oil
2 c. hot water (125°)
5 ½ c. flour
Cooking spray

Yield:
2 loaves

Serving Size:
1 slice

Preparation Time:
30 minutes

Rising Time:
75 minutes

Cooking Time:
30–40 minutes

Soften yeast in ¼–½ cup warm water; let stand 5 minutes. Combine rye flour, molasses, brown sugar, caraway seeds, and oil; pour hot water over rye mixture and mix well. Add yeast and 3 cups white flour; stir well. Continue to add white flour until a soft dough forms. Turn dough out onto a floured surface and knead 10 minutes. Cover and let rise about 1 hour until doubled in bulk. Punch dough down and divide in half. Shape loaves and put them into two 9 x 5 x 2-inch loaf pans coated with cooking spray. Let the loaves rise again to no more than double, about 30 minutes. Bake in a 350° oven for about 30–40 minutes or until loaves sound hollow when tapped. (The loaves should be golden brown.)

All whole-wheat bread is brown but not all brown bread is whole-wheat. Raisin juice is often added to bread to darken the color and create the illusion that it is a whole-wheat product.

Nutrition Analysis Per Serving:

Calories 158

Protein 4g

Carbohydrate 33g

Fat 1g

(Saturated <1g)

Cholesterol 0mg

Fiber 2g

Sodium 294mg

Quick Yeast Rolls

Rapid-rise yeast makes this recipe a snap!

Yield:
16 servings

Serving Size:
1 roll

Preparation Time:
30 minutes

Rising Time:
30 minutes

Cooking Time:
20–25 minutes

3 ½–4 c. flour, divided
1 pkg. rapid-rise yeast
¼ c. sugar
1 tsp. salt
1 c. water
1 ½ T. canola oil
1 egg
Cooking spray

Set aside one cup of flour for later use. In a large bowl, combine remaining flour, yeast, sugar, and salt. In microwave, heat water and oil until hot to touch (105–115°). Stir hot liquids into dry mixture. Mix in egg. Knead in enough of the reserved flour so that the dough is no longer sticky. Cover dough and let rest for 10 minutes. Shape dough into 16 rolls and place them in two 9-inch round pans coated with cooking spray. Let rise until doubled in bulk (about 30 minutes). Bake at 350° for 20–25 minutes or until golden brown.

Nutrition Analysis Per Serving:

Calories 128

Protein 3g

Carbohydrate 24g

Fat 2g

(Saturated <1 g)

Cholesterol 13mg

Fiber 1g

Sodium 151mg

Breads made with quick-rising yeast rise in a third less time than traditional yeast breads. Quick-rising yeast can replace active dry yeast in all recipes except Danish pastry, croissants, and anything made with a sourdough starter.

Honey Whole-wheat Bread

This is a heavy, flavorful bread—delicious for toast and sandwiches.

2 pkgs. rapid-rise yeast
1 qt. warm skim milk (105–115°)
3 T. honey
3 T. oil
1 tsp. salt
8–8 ½ c. whole-wheat flour
Cooking spray

Soften yeast in warm milk in a large mixing bowl; let stand 5 minutes. Add honey, oil, and salt. Gradually add flour, 1 cup at a time, to make a soft dough. Cover and let rise in a warm place for 1 hour or until doubled in bulk. Turn dough out onto a floured surface and knead until smooth and elastic (about 10 minutes). Divide dough in half and place in two 9 x 5 x 3-inch loaf pans coated with cooking spray. Cover and let rise in a warm place for 30 minutes. Bake at 350° for 40–45 minutes or until loaf sounds hollow when tapped.

By law, bread that is labeled "whole-wheat" must be made from 100% whole-wheat flour. Stone-ground wheat bread, cracked wheat bread, and wheat bread do not contain the term "whole" in their names and may be made from varying portions of enriched white flour and whole-wheat flour.

Yield:
2 loaves

Serving Size:
1 slice

Preparation Time:
20 minutes

Rising Time:
100 minutes

Cooking time:
40–45 minutes

Nutrition Analysis Per Serving:

Calories 124

Protein 5g

Carbohydrate 22g

Fat 2g

(Saturated <1g)

Cholesterol <1mg

Fiber 3g

Sodium 71mg

Dilly Casserole Bread

Delicious served warm with Winter Stew (p. 72).

Yield:
1 loaf

Serving Size:
1 slice

Preparation Time:
5–10 minutes

Rising Time:
90 minutes

Cooking Time:
40–50 minutes

Nutrition Analysis Per Serving:

Calories 134

Protein 6g

Carbohydrate 23g

Fat 2g

(Saturated 1g)

Cholesterol 18mg

Fiber 1g

Sodium 314mg

1 pkg. rapid-rise yeast
¼ c. warm water (105–115°)
1 c. 1% cottage cheese
2 T. sugar
1 T. margarine, melted
1 T. dried onion flakes
2 tsp. dill seeds
1 tsp. salt
¼ tsp. baking soda
1 egg, beaten
2 ½ c. flour
Cooking spray

Soften yeast in warm water in a large mixing bowl; let stand 5 minutes. Combine cottage cheese, sugar, margarine, onion flakes, dill seeds, salt, baking soda, and egg; stir until blended. Stir yeast into cottage cheese mixture; gradually stir in flour to make a soft dough. Cover and let rise in a warm place for 50 minutes, or until doubled in bulk. Punch dough down and place in a 2-quart round casserole coated with cooking spray. Cover and let rise in a warm place 40 minutes. Bake at 350° for 40–50 minutes or until golden brown.

The microwave oven makes a great "warm place" for rising yeast bread. Heat one cup of water for two minutes on full power in the microwave. Remove water and place covered dough inside oven to rise.

Mexican Cornbread

Serve this bread fresh from the oven with a steaming bowl of Gringo Chili (p. 76)—there's nothing better after a day of cross-country skiing.

1 ½ c. cornmeal
¾ tsp. salt
½ tsp. baking soda
1 c. lowfat buttermilk
2 egg whites
1 egg
1 can (16 ½ oz.) cream-style corn
1 c. shredded reduced-fat
sharp Cheddar cheese
1 large onion, chopped
1 clove garlic, minced
1 can (4 oz.) chopped green chiles
2 T. margarine, melted
Cooking spray

Yield:
12 servings

Serving Size:
3 ¼ x 3-inch piece

Preparation Time:
5–10 minutes

Cooking Time:
45 minutes

Preheat oven to 350°. Combine cornmeal, salt, and baking soda. Stir in buttermilk and remaining ingredients. Spoon into a 13 x 9 x 2-inch baking dish lightly coated with cooking spray and sprinkled with cornmeal. Bake 45 minutes or until a wooden pick inserted in center comes out clean. Let cool 5 minutes before serving.

Nutrition Analysis Per Serving:

Calories 159

Protein 6g

Carbohydrate 23g

Fat 5g

(*Saturated 2g*)

Cholesterol 25mg

Fiber 2g

Sodium 424mg

To lower the cholesterol in your recipes, substitute two egg whites for each whole egg that you replace.

Bran Muffin Starter

Fresh muffins every morning are a breeze with this recipe.

Yield:
60 servings

Serving Size:
1 muffin

Preparation Time:
15–20 minutes

Cooking Time:
20 minutes

2 c. boiling water
2 c. shredded whole-bran cereal
5 c. flour
5 tsp. baking soda
2 tsp. salt
2 c. sugar
1 c. margarine, softened
1 c. egg substitute
1 qt. lowfat buttermilk
4 c. whole-bran cereal buds
Cooking spray

Nutrition Analysis Per Serving:

Calories 120

Protein 3g

Carbohydrate 22g

Fat 4g

(Saturated 1g)

Cholesterol 1mg

Fiber 3g

Sodium 295mg

Pour boiling water over shredded whole bran cereal; set aside. Sift together flour, baking soda, and salt. Cream together sugar and margarine in a large mixing bowl until light and fluffy. Add egg substitute and beat well. Blend in buttermilk, bran-cereal buds, and the soaked whole-bran cereal. Stir in dry ingredients until moistened. Store in a tightly covered container in refrigerator. Batter will keep for up to 6 weeks.

To make muffins, preheat oven to 400°. Lightly coat a standard muffin pan with cooking spray. Fill cups ⅔ full with batter (don't stir batter). Bake for 20 minutes or until done.

Because egg substitutes are pasteurized, there is no danger of them containing salmonella. That's why we used them in the Make-Ahead recipe. Plus, egg substitutes are lower in cholesterol than whole eggs.

Oatmeal-Blueberry Muffins

1 c. flour
1 ½ c. quick-cooking oats, uncooked
1 tsp. cinnamon
1 tsp. baking powder
½ tsp. baking soda
¼ tsp. salt
1 c. lowfat buttermilk
½ c. packed brown sugar
¼ c. oil
1 egg, beaten
1 c. frozen blueberries
2 T. brown sugar

Yield:
18 servings

Serving Size:
1 muffin

Preparation Time:
10–15 minutes

Cooking Time:
20–25 minutes

Preheat oven to 425°. Combine flour, oats, cinnamon, baking powder, baking soda, and salt; set aside. Combine buttermilk, ½ cup brown sugar, oil, and egg in a medium mixing bowl; add to flour mixture, mixing just until moist. Fold in blueberries. Fill paper-lined muffin cups ⅔ full with batter; sprinkle with remaining 2 tablespoons brown sugar. Bake 20–25 minutes or until done.

If you don't have buttermilk on hand when you need it for baking, use this easy substitute: For each cup of buttermilk, place one tablespoon of lemon juice or vinegar in a glass measuring cup and add enough cold milk to make one cup; stir and let stand five minutes before using.

Nutrition Analysis Per Serving:

Calories 120

Protein 3g

Carbohydrate 19g

Fat 4g

(Saturated <1g)

Cholesterol 12mg

Fiber 2g

Sodium 116mg

Trail Ride Zucchini Muffins

A great breakfast muffin for the trail.

Yield:
18 servings

Serving Size:
1 muffin

Preparation Time:
15 minutes

Cooking Time:
20 minutes

1 c. whole-wheat flour
1 c. flour
2 tsp. baking soda
¼ tsp. baking powder
1 T. cinnamon
1 egg, beaten
⅓ c. oil
¾ c. sugar
½ c. nonfat dry milk
2 ½ c. grated zucchini
2 tsp. vanilla
1 tsp. lemon extract
½ c. raisins
¼ c. chopped nuts
Cooking spray

Nutrition Analysis Per Serving:

Calories 164

Protein 3g

Carbohydrate 24g

Fat 6g

(Saturated 1g)

Cholesterol 12mg

Fiber 2g

Sodium 163mg

Preheat oven to 350°. Sift flours, soda, baking powder, and cinnamon together in a bowl; set aside. Combine egg, oil, sugar, dry milk, zucchini, vanilla, and lemon extract in another bowl; beat thoroughly. Stir egg mixture into flour mixture just until smooth. Stir in raisins and nuts. Lightly spray a standard-size muffin pan. Fill muffin cups ⅔ full with batter. Bake for 20 minutes or until done.

Leftover bran muffins make an excellent breakfast sundae. Crumble them in a bowl and top with lowfat yogurt and fresh fruit.

Honey-Lemon Muffins

2 c. flour
2 ½ tsp. baking powder
½ tsp. baking soda
½ tsp. salt
1 T. grated lemon peel
1 egg
¼ c. oil
⅓ c. honey
1 c. plain nonfat or lowfat yogurt
2 T. lemon juice
Cooking spray

Preheat oven to 400°. Combine flour,
baking powder, baking soda, salt, and
grated lemon peel; set aside. Mix egg, oil,
honey, yogurt, and lemon juice; add to dry
ingredients, stirring just until moistened.
Fill standard-size muffin cups lightly coated
with cooking spray to ⅔ full with batter.
Bake for 18 minutes or until golden brown.

Yield:
12 servings

Serving Size:
1 muffin

Preparation Time:
20 minutes

Cooking Time:
18 minutes

**Nutrition Analysis
Per Serving:**

Calories 160

Protein 4g

Carbohydrate 26g

Fat 5g

(Saturated <1g)

Cholesterol 18mg

Fiber 1g

Sodium 269mg

Mountain Biker's Banana Muffins

Put these in your pack for a tasty snack while biking.

Yield:
12 servings

Serving Size:
1 muffin

Preparation Time:
15–20 minutes

Cooking Time:
15–20 minutes

½ c. sugar
1 tsp. baking soda
¼ tsp. salt
¾ c. flour
¾ c. whole-wheat flour
⅓ c. oil
¼ c. skim milk
2 large bananas, mashed
1 tsp. vanilla
⅓ c. raisins
Cooking spray

Preheat oven to 375º. Measure sugar, baking soda, salt, and flours into bowl. Add oil, milk, bananas, and vanilla; mix just until flour is moistened. Fold in raisins. Fill standard-size muffin cups coated with cooking spray to ⅔ full with batter. Bake 15–20 minutes or until golden brown. Remove from pan immediately.

Nutrition Analysis Per Serving:

Calories 179

Protein 3g

Carbohydrate 29g

Fat 6g

(Saturated <1g)

Cholesterol <1mg

Fiber 2g

Sodium 157mg

Fresh Raspberry Muffins

Mouthwatering, delicious, and unbelievably yummy!

1 ¼ c. fresh raspberries
1 ½ c. flour, divided
⅓ c. packed brown sugar
2 tsp. baking powder
1 tsp. cinnamon
¼ tsp. salt
1 egg, beaten
¼ c. oil
½ c. skim milk
Cooking spray

Topping:
3 T. nuts, chopped
2 T. brown sugar
1 tsp. cinnamon
⅓ c. powdered sugar
2 tsp. lemon juice

Preheat oven to 350°. Dust raspberries with 2 tablespoons of flour; set aside. Combine remaining flour, sugar, baking powder, 1 tsp. cinnamon, and salt. In a separate bowl, combine egg, oil, and milk. Add flour mixture to egg mixture alternately with milk mixture. Fold in raspberries. Lightly spray a standard-size muffin pan with cooking spray. Fill muffin cups ⅔ full with batter. Combine nuts, brown sugar, and 1 tsp. cinnamon; sprinkle over muffins and bake 20–25 minutes. Stir together powdered sugar and lemon juice. When muffins are slightly cooled, drizzle lemon juice mixture over muffins.

Yield:
12 servings

Serving Size:
1 muffin

Preparation Time:
25 minutes

Cooking Time:
25 minutes

Nutrition Analysis Per Serving:

Calories 173

Protein 3g

Carbohydrate 26g

Fat 7g

(Saturated 1g)

Cholesterol 18mg

Fiber 2g

Sodium 144mg

Banana-Chocolate Chip Muffins

Yield:
12 servings

Serving Size:
1 muffin

Preparation Time:
15–20 minutes

Cooking Time:
20–25 minutes

1 c. flour
¾ c. whole-wheat flour
⅓ c. packed brown sugar
1 tsp. baking powder
½ tsp. baking soda
1 c. mashed bananas (about 2 bananas)
½ c. plain nonfat or lowfat yogurt
1 egg
1 egg white
2 T. canola oil
½ c. miniature chocolate chips

Nutrition Analysis Per Serving:

Calories 189

Protein 4g

Carbohydrate 31g

Fat 6g

(Saturated 2g)

Cholesterol 18mg

Fiber 2g

Sodium 112mg

Preheat oven to 375°. Line 12 muffin cups with paper liners or coat with cooking spray. Combine the flour, whole-wheat flour, brown sugar, baking powder, and baking soda in a bowl and mix well. Combine the bananas, yogurt, egg, egg white, and canola oil in a bowl and mix well. Add banana mixture to the flour mixture, stirring just until moistened. Fold in the chocolate chips. Fill the muffin cups ⅔ full. Bake 20–25 minutes or until a wooden pick inserted in the center comes out clean. Remove muffins and let cool on a wire rack.

Using miniature chocolate chips is a great way to include chocolate in your recipes. Because they are small, the chocolate chips disperse well in batters. For most recipes, you can cut the amount of chocolate chips in half and still enjoy that rich chocolate flavor.

Fruit Scones

3 c. flour
2 ½ tsp. baking powder
¼ c. sugar
½ tsp. baking soda
½ tsp. salt
¼ c. butter
1 ¼ c. lowfat buttermilk
1 c. any dried fruit, chopped
Cooking spray
1 T. sugar

Preheat the oven to 450°. Combine the flour,
baking powder, ¼ c. sugar, baking soda,
and salt in a bowl and mix well. Cut in the
butter with a pastry blender or 2 knives
until crumbly. Add the buttermilk and dried
fruit, stirring until the mixture adheres and
forms a ball. Place the dough on a baking
sheet coated with cooking spray. Pat into a
¾-inch-thick circle. Score the dough into 12
wedges with a sharp knife. Sprinkle with 1
tablespoon sugar. Bake for 25 minutes or until
a wooden pick inserted into the center comes
out clean. Cool slightly. Cut into 12 wedges.

Yield:
12 servings

Serving Size:
1 scone

Preparation Time:
15 minutes

Cooking Time:
25 minutes

**Nutrition Analysis
Per Serving:**

Calories 206

Protein 5g

Carbohydrate 38g

Fat 4g

(Saturated 3g)

Cholesterol 11mg

Fiber 2g

Sodium 319mg

Orange-Cranberry Scones

Yield:
12 servings

Serving Size:
1 scone

Preparation Time:
15 minutes

Cooking Time:
12–15 minutes

1 ⅓ c. flour
⅔ c. rolled oats
¼ c. sugar
1 tsp. baking powder
½ tsp. baking soda
½ tsp. salt
Grated zest of 1 orange
3 T. butter or margarine
½ c. lowfat buttermilk
3 oz. dried cranberries
2 T. orange juice

Preheat oven to 425°. Combine the flour, oats, sugar, baking powder, baking soda, salt, and zest in a bowl and mix well. Cut in the butter with a pastry blender or 2 knives until crumbly. Combine the buttermilk, cranberries, and orange juice in a bowl and mix well. Stir into the flour mixture with a fork. Knead the dough on a lightly floured surface 8–10 times. Divide the dough into 2 equal portions. Shape each portion into a ball and pat the balls into ½-inch-thick circles. Cut each circle into 6 wedges. Arrange the wedges 1 inch apart on a baking sheet. Bake for 12–15 minutes or until light brown.

Nutrition Analysis Per Serving:

Calories 139

Protein 3g

Carbohydrate 24g

Fat 3g

(Saturated 2g)

Cholesterol 8mg

Fiber 2g

Sodium 231mg

Vegetarian Entrées

Cranberry-Glazed Tempeh

If you like tempeh, you will love this recipe.

Yield:
4 servings

Serving Size:
4 ounces
(2 triangles)

Preparation Time:
15–20 minutes

Cooking Time:
50–55 minutes

2 pkgs. (8 oz. each) wild rice tempeh
1 can (15 oz.) whole cranberry sauce
½ c. water
2 T. maple syrup
1 T. soy sauce
1 T. dry sherry
1 T. grated fresh ginger root,
or 1 tsp. ground ginger
¼ tsp. allspice
¼ tsp. cinnamon
¼ tsp. salt
⅛ tsp. nutmeg
Cayenne pepper, to taste

Preheat oven to 350°. Cut each block of tempeh into 4 triangles. Steam the tempeh in a steamer basket for 10 minutes. Arrange in a single layer in a baking dish. Combine the cranberry sauce, water, maple syrup, soy sauce, sherry, ginger root, allspice, cinnamon, salt, nutmeg, and cayenne pepper in a blender or food processor. Process until smooth. Strain the sauce through fine mesh strainer to remove the seeds, for a smoother sauce. Pour over the tempeh. Bake for 40–45 minutes.

Tempeh is a flat cake made from fermented soybeans. Unlike tofu, which absorbs the flavors of the foods with which it is cooked, tempeh has a smoky flavor and a chewy texture. Here are some suggestions: Grill tempeh after marinating it in a sauce; chop tempeh and mix it in casseroles, chili, or soups; or grill tempeh and top it with burger fixings.

Nutrition Analysis Per Serving:

Calories 409

Protein 22g

Carbohydrate 66g

Fat 9g

(Saturated 1g)

Cholesterol 0mg

Fiber 8g

Sodium 505mg

Grilled Tofu Steaks

1 lb. firm tofu, cut lengthwise into 4 steaks
¼ c. low-sodium soy sauce
¼ c. red wine vinegar
1 tsp. olive oil
1 tsp. sesame oil
½ tsp. dried oregano leaves
¼ tsp. garlic powder
⅛ tsp. ground ginger
Cayenne pepper, to taste

Place the tofu on a plate lined with paper towels. Cover the tofu with additional paper towels. Top with a plate. Weight with several canned goods or a cast-iron skillet to press out excess moisture. Let stand for 20 minutes. Combine the soy sauce, wine vinegar, olive oil, sesame oil, oregano, garlic powder, ginger, and pepper in a shallow dish and mix well. Add the tofu steaks, turning to coat. Marinate, covered, in the refrigerator for 6 hours or longer, turning once; drain. Grill over medium-hot coals for 6 minutes per side or until brown. May broil if desired. Serve with rice or another whole grain for a filling meal.

Pressing the moisture out of the tofu allows it to become firm and absorb flavors in the sauce.

Yield:
4 servings

Serving Size:
1 steak

Preparation Time:
10 minutes

Marinating Time:
6 hours

Cooking Time:
12 minutes

Nutrition Analysis Per Serving:

Calories 110

Protein 9g

Carbohydrate 5g

Fat 5g

(Saturated 1g)

Cholesterol 0mg

Fiber <1g

Sodium 547mg

Vegetable Tofu Curry

Yield:
5 servings

Serving Size:
1 cup

Preparation Time:
25 minutes

Cooking Time:
40 minutes

3 c. water
3 potatoes, peeled and cubed
3 carrots, cut into ¼-inch slices
1 tsp. salt
1 ½ T. canola oil
1 large onion, chopped
1 large apple, sliced
⅓ c. raisins
8 oz. firm tofu, cubed
2 T. flour
2 T. curry powder
1 ½ tsp. cinnamon
2 tsp. low-sodium soy sauce

Bring the water to a boil in a 4-quart saucepan. Add the potatoes, carrots, and salt. Cook for 15 minutes or until the vegetables are tender. Drain, reserving the vegetable broth. Return the vegetables to the saucepan. Cover to keep warm. Heat the canola oil in a large skillet over medium-high heat. Add the onion. Sauté for 5 minutes or until tender; reduce heat. Stir in the apple and raisins.

Cook over low heat for 10 minutes, stirring occasionally. Add the tofu and mix well. Cook for 5 minutes, stirring frequently. Sprinkle the flour, curry powder, and cinnamon over the tofu mixture and mix well. Stir in the reserved vegetable broth and soy sauce. Cook until thickened, stirring constantly. Add to the potatoes and carrots and mix gently. Serve over hot cooked basmati rice, with chutney on the side.

Nutrition Analysis Per Serving:

Calories 227

Protein 7g

Carbohydrate 39g

Fat 6g

(*Saturated 1g*)

Cholesterol 0mg

Fiber 5g

Sodium 572mg

Telluride Tofu & Mushrooms

Mushrooms provide a meaty texture for this meatless dish.

4 c. hot cooked rice
1 lb. firm tofu
½ c. low-sodium soy sauce
1 T. brown sugar
1 T. olive oil
2 c. sliced fresh mushrooms
2 cloves garlic, minced
1 large tomato, chopped
¼ c. chopped green onions

Yield:
4 servings

Serving Size:
1 cup rice and ½ cup stir-fry

Preparation Time:
20–25 minutes

Cooking Time:
10 minutes

Prepare rice according to package directions, and set aside. Place the tofu block on a plate lined with paper towels. Cover the tofu with additional paper towels. Top with a plate. Weight with several canned goods or a cast-iron skillet to press out excess moisture. Let stand for 20 minutes. Combine the soy sauce and brown sugar in a small bowl and mix well. Heat the olive oil in a large non-stick skillet. Add the mushrooms and garlic. Sauté over medium heat until the mushrooms are tender. Cut the tofu into ½-inch cubes. Stir into the mushroom mixture. Add the soy sauce mixture, tomato, and green onions and mix well. Cook for 5 minutes, stirring frequently. Spoon over the rice on a serving platter.

Firm and extra-firm tofu hold their texture and shape and are best in salads, stir-fry, and in recipes that call for meat or chicken. Soft tofu is moist and can be used for dressings and dips, or as a substitute for soft cheeses, such as ricotta.

Nutrition Analysis Per Serving:

Calories 370

Protein 16g

Carbohydrate 60g

Fat 7g

(Saturated 1g)

Cholesterol 0mg

Fiber 2g

Sodium 1061mg

Mesa Verde Black Beans with Rice

Yield:
6 servings

Serving Size:
1 cup

Preparation Time:
15–20 minutes

Cooking Time:
30 minutes

Nutrition Analysis Per Serving:

Calories 332

Protein 12g

Carbohydrate 75g

Fat <1g

(Saturated <1g)

Cholesterol <1mg

Fiber 9g

Sodium 414mg

4 ½ c. cooked long-grain rice
Cooking spray
1 c. chopped onion
1 c. chopped green bell pepper
4 cloves garlic, minced
2 cans (15 oz. each) black beans, drained
2 c. water
¼ tsp. crushed red pepper flakes
¼ tsp. salt
1 can (6 oz.) tomato paste
1 T. vinegar
½ c. chopped tomatoes
¼ c. chopped green onions
¼ c. plain nonfat or lowfat yogurt

Prepare long-grain rice according to package directions; set aside. Coat a large pot with cooking spray. Place over medium heat; add onion, green pepper, and garlic; sauté until tender, stirring often. Add black beans, water, crushed red pepper flakes, and salt. Bring to a boil; cover, reduce heat, and simmer 15 minutes, stirring occasionally. Add tomato paste and vinegar; uncover and cook 15 minutes longer or until thickened. Serve over ¾ cup rice and top evenly with chopped tomatoes, green onions, and yogurt.

The acid in tomatoes and vinegar toughens beans—that's why these ingredients usually are added last.

Boulder Burritos

These make a great grab-and-go meal, and are an adventurous way to add more greens to your diet.

1 c. water
½ c. bulgur
1 large onion, chopped
4 cloves garlic, minced
3 T. olive oil
6 c. chopped kale
1 can (15 oz.) pinto beans, drained and rinsed
2 T. lemon juice
2 tsp. cumin
8 (10-inch) flour tortillas
1 c. your favorite salsa
1 c. shredded, reduced-fat Cheddar cheese

Yield:
8 servings

Serving Size:
1 burrito

Preparation Time:
20–25 minutes

Cooking Time:
40 minutes

Combine water and bulgur in a saucepan and mix well. Simmer for 20 minutes or until tender. In a skillet, sauté the onion and garlic in olive oil until tender. Stir in the kale and sauté until wilted. Add bulgur, beans, lemon juice, and cumin; mix well. Cook until heated through, stirring occasionally. Remove from heat. Spoon ⅛ of the bean mixture onto each tortilla. Top each with 2 tablespoons of the salsa and 2 tablespoons of the cheese. Roll to enclose the filling. Arrange seam side down in a 9 x 13 x 2-inch baking dish. Bake, covered, at 350° for 15 minutes or until heated through—or microwave on medium for 3 to 4 minutes.

To please vegetarians and non-vegetarians alike, center meals around entrées that are not typically thought of as vegetarian, such as soups and sandwiches, pasta with marinara sauce, macaroni and cheese, vegetable "fried" rice, or bean burritos.

Nutrition Analysis Per Serving:

Calories 423

Protein 16g

Carbohydrate 64g

Fat 12g

(Saturated 3g)

Cholesterol 3mg

Fiber 8g

Sodium 751mg

Black Bean Tortilla Casserole

Yield:
6 servings

Serving Size:
4 ½ x 4 ½-inch piece

Preparation Time:
25 minutes

Cooking Time:
50 minutes

Nutrition Analysis Per Serving:

Calories 389

Protein 22g

Carbohydrate 57g

Fat 9g

(Saturated 4g)

Cholesterol 20mg

Fiber 14g

Sodium 942mg

Cooking spray
1 c. chopped onion
2 c. chopped red and green bell peppers
2 cloves garlic, minced
2 cans (15 oz.) black beans, drained and rinsed
1 can (14 oz.) no-salt-added diced tomatoes, undrained
1 c. your favorite picante sauce
1 T. cumin
12 (6-inch) corn tortillas
1 ½ c. shredded, reduced-fat Monterey Jack cheese
2 c. shredded lettuce
½ c. chopped tomato
⅓ c. light sour cream

Spray a large, non-stick skillet with cooking spray. Sauté onion; add bell peppers and garlic and mix well. Sauté for 3 minutes or until peppers are tender. Stir in beans, undrained tomatoes, picante sauce, and cumin. Cook for 5 minutes, stirring occasionally. Remove from heat.

Lightly coat a 9 x 13 x 2-inch baking pan with cooking spray. Spread 1 cup bean mixture in pan. Arrange 6 tortillas over bean mixture. Spread with ¾ cup cheese. Spoon 2 ½ cups bean mixture over cheese. Top with 6 more tortillas and add remaining bean mixture. Bake, covered, at 350° for 30 minutes; sprinkle with remaining ¾ cup cheese. Bake until cheese melts. Let stand for 5 minutes before serving then cut into 6 portions. Top with lettuce, tomato, and sour cream.

Spinach Enchilada Casserole

1 medium onion, chopped
Cooking spray
1 pkg. (10 oz.) frozen chopped spinach, thawed
2 cans (8 oz. each) tomato sauce
1 can (12 oz.) mexicorn, drained
1 can (10 oz.) mild enchilada sauce
1 tsp. chili powder
¼ tsp. dried oregano leaves
12 corn tortillas
6 oz. shredded part-skim mozzarella cheese
1 c. shredded lettuce
½ c. chopped fresh tomatoes

Yield:
8 servings

Serving Size:
4 ½ x 3 ¼-inch piece

Preparation Time:
25 minutes

Cooking Time:
25 minutes

Preheat oven to 350°. Sauté onion in a large non-stick skillet coated with cooking spray. Drain spinach and pat out excess moisture between paper towels. In a saucepan, combine onion, spinach, tomato sauce, mexicorn, enchilada sauce, and seasonings; mix well. Bring to a boil; reduce heat and simmer for 5 minutes. Place 6 tortillas in the bottom of a 9 x 13 x 2-inch baking dish.

Pour half of spinach mixture over tortillas; sprinkle with one-half of mozzarella cheese. Repeat the layers, using tortillas and spinach mixture. Bake for 20 minutes. Sprinkle with remaining mozzarella cheese and bake an additional 5 minutes. Garnish with lettuce and tomato. (If prepared ahead of time, refrigerate covered. Allow 40 minutes heating time; sprinkle with mozzarella cheese during last 5 minutes of baking.)

Nutrition Analysis Per Serving:

Calories 184

Protein 10g

Carbohydrate 26g

Fat 5g

(Saturated 2g)

Cholesterol 14mg

Fiber 3g

Sodium 805mg

Spinach Quesadillas

Yield:
4 servings

Serving Size:
1 quesadilla

Preparation Time:
15–20 minutes

Cooking Time:
25 minutes

1 pkg. (10 oz.) frozen chopped spinach
2 T. minced onion
2 T. minced garlic
2 T. minced mushrooms
2 T. minced fresh jalapeño chiles
2 T. minced fresh cilantro
8 (6-inch) corn tortillas
Cooking spray
4 oz. fat-free or regular refried beans
¼ c. shredded mozzarella cheese
Salsa Fresca, (p. 10)

Combine the spinach with a small amount of water in a microwave-safe dish. Microwave, covered, on high for 5 minutes or until the spinach is thawed; drain. Squeeze the excess moisture from the spinach by placing it between paper towels and gently patting it down. Combine the spinach, onion, garlic, mushrooms, chiles, and cilantro in a bowl and mix well.

Arrange 4 of the tortillas in a single layer on a baking sheet coated with cooking spray. Spread the tortillas with the refried beans. Spread with the spinach mixture and sprinkle with cheese. Top with the remaining tortillas. Bake at 375° for 15–20 minutes or until light brown. Serve with salsa.

Variation: Try making these with *Santa Fe Beans,* (p. 147).

Nutrition Analysis Per Serving:

Calories 200

Protein 9g

Carbohydrate 37g

Fat 3g

(Saturated 1g)

Cholesterol 6mg

Fiber 7g

Sodium 274mg

Twice-Baked Potato Dinner

Bake extra potatoes to have them ready for this scrumptious entrée.

2 large potatoes, baked
6 T. skim milk
½ c. 1% cottage cheese
¼ c. chopped green pepper
¼ c. chopped carrots
¼ c. chopped green onions
2 T. sunflower seeds
½ c. shredded reduced-fat
sharp Cheddar cheese
¼ tsp. garlic salt
¼ tsp. black pepper
6 cherry tomatoes, halved

Yield:
4 servings

Serving Size:
½ potato

Preparation Time:
20 minutes

Cooking Time:
10–12 minutes

Preheat oven to 450°. Halve the baked potatoes and scoop out pulp, leaving ¼ inch remaining in shells. Mash potato pulp in a bowl. Add milk, cottage cheese, green pepper, carrot, onion, sunflower seeds, half the Cheddar cheese, salt, and pepper. Gently mix to blend thoroughly. Mound into potato shells, dividing equally. Arrange 3 cherry tomato halves on each potato half, pushing them in slightly. Sprinkle with remaining Cheddar cheese. Bake for 10–12 minutes or until cheese is melted and potatoes are heated thoroughly.

Hint: Potatoes may be prepared in advance up to the point of heating. Wrap them securely and refrigerate up to 2 days. Reheat in a conventional oven, as directed above, or heat them in a microwave, according to manufacturer's directions.

Nutrition Analysis Per Serving:

Calories 202

Protein 11g

Carbohydrate 27g

Fat 6g

(*Saturated 2g*)

Cholesterol 9mg

Fiber 3g

Sodium 304mg

Sesame Chick-Pea Dinner Wraps

Yield:
6 servings

Serving Size:
1 wrap

Preparation Time:
15 minutes

2 T. sesame seeds
1 can (15 oz.) chick-peas, drained and rinsed
6 c. slivered romaine lettuce
1 red bell pepper, finely chopped
4 oz. reduced-fat feta cheese, crumbled
3 T. lemon juice
1 T. olive oil
1 T. chopped fresh basil, or 1 tsp. dried basil
1 tsp. minced garlic
½ tsp. freshly ground black pepper
6 (10-inch) flour tortillas, heated

Toast the sesame seeds in an ungreased skillet over medium heat until golden brown and fragrant, stirring frequently. Process the chick-peas in a blender or food processor until coarsely chopped. Toss romaine and red pepper in a salad bowl. Add the feta cheese and chick peas and mix well. Sprinkle with sesame seeds. Whisk the lemon juice, olive oil, basil, garlic, and pepper in a bowl. Drizzle over the romaine mixture, tossing to coat. Spoon 1 cup of the romaine mixture in the center of each tortilla. Roll to enclose the filling.

**Nutrition Analysis
Per Serving:**

Calories 423

Protein 14g

Carbohydrate 61g

Fat 14g

(*Saturated 5g*)

Cholesterol 17mg

Fiber 7g

Sodium 773mg

Sesame seeds and olive oil are good sources of monounsaturated fats, which help lower blood cholesterol levels.

Vegetable Calzones

1 loaf (1 lb.) frozen bread dough,
white or whole-wheat
2 tsp. olive oil
1 c. sliced fresh mushrooms
¾ c. chopped red bell pepper
½ c. chopped onion
1 pkg. (10 oz.) frozen chopped spinach, thawed
1 c. light ricotta cheese
¼ c. grated Parmesan cheese
1 c. (4 oz.) shredded part-
skim mozzarella cheese
½ tsp. Italian seasoning
Cooking spray
2 c. your favorite spaghetti sauce

Yield:
4 servings

Serving Size:
1 calzone

Preparation Time:
30 minutes

Cooking Time:
15–20 minutes

Let bread dough rise according to package directions. Preheat oven to 400°. Heat olive oil in a nonstick skillet over medium heat; add mushrooms, red pepper, and onion. Sauté until tender; remove from heat. Drain spinach and squeeze out excess moisture. Combine spinach, cheeses, and Italian seasoning; mix well. Add sautéed vegetables and mix well.

Punch bread dough down and divide into 4 equal portions. Shape each portion into an 8-inch circle. Spoon ⅔ cup vegetable and cheese mixture onto ½ of each circle, leaving a ½-inch border. Moisten edges of circle with water. Fold plain half of each circle over filling, crimping edges to seal. Place calzones on baking sheet coated with cooking spray. Bake 15–20 minutes or until golden brown. Serve with ½ c. spaghetti sauce for dipping.

Nutrition Analysis Per Serving:

Calories 631

Protein 33g

Carbohydrate 79g

Fat 22g

(Saturated 6g)

Cholesterol 24mg

Fiber 8g

Sodium 1526mg

Portobello Mushroom Sandwiches

Yield:
4 servings

Serving Size:
1 sandwich

Preparation Time:
10 minutes

Marinating Time:
20–30 minutes

Cooking Time:
10 minutes

**Nutrition Analysis
Per Serving:**

Calories 410

Protein 18g

Carbohydrate 58g

Fat 13g

(Saturated 5g)

Cholesterol 15mg

Fiber 8g

Sodium 856mg

½ c. balsamic vinegar
¼ c. Worcestershire sauce
2 green onions, finely chopped
1 T. olive oil
1 tsp. crushed dried rosemary
4 Portobello mushrooms, stems removed
4 Kaiser rolls, split
2 oz. goat or feta cheese, crumbled
⅓ c. roasted red bell pepper slices
1 c. fresh spinach leaves

Combine the balsamic vinegar, Worcestershire sauce, green onions, olive oil, and rosemary in a sealable plastic bag. Add the mushrooms and seal tightly. Toss to coat. Marinate at room temperature for 20–30 minutes, turning occasionally; drain. Grill the mushrooms over medium-hot coals for 4–6 minutes per side. Place the rolls on the grill rack. Grill for 2–3 minutes. Layer the cheese, mushroom caps, red pepper, and spinach (in the order listed) on the bottom roll halves. Top with the remaining roll halves. Serve with a salad of mixed greens.

Roasting peppers is easily done individually or in quantity. To roast a single pepper, secure the pepper with a long-handled fork or skewer. Turn a stove-top burner to high and rotate the pepper until it is evenly charred. Place the pepper in a paper bag and seal tightly. When cooled, remove the charred skin. To roast several peppers, broil in oven or toaster oven, turning frequently. Or grill the peppers over hot coals until charred and blistered.

Portobello Mushrooms Florentine

4 whole Portobello mushrooms,
stems and black "ribs" removed
½ tsp. olive oil
1 pkg. (10 oz.) frozen chopped
spinach, thawed and drained
¼ c. chopped onion
3 T. dry breadcrumbs
2 tsp. grated Parmesan cheese
1 tsp. garlic powder
1 tsp. dried oregano leaves
1 egg, lightly beaten
¼ c. shredded mozzarella cheese

Yield:
4 servings

Serving Size:
1 mushroom cap

Preparation Time:
20 minutes

Cooking Time:
25–30 minutes

Arrange the mushrooms with top sides down
on a baking sheet. Heat the olive oil in a large
non-stick skillet over medium heat. Add the
spinach and onion and mix well. Sauté for 10
minutes or until the onion is tender. Stir in the
breadcrumbs, Parmesan cheese, garlic powder,
and oregano. Remove from heat. Stir in the egg.
Spoon equal portions of the spinach mixture
onto each mushroom and pat firmly. Top each
with 1 tablespoon of mozzarella cheese. Bake at
375° for 15–20 minutes or until light brown.

**Nutrition Analysis
Per Serving:**

Calories 139

Protein 14g

Carbohydrate 18g

Fat 4g

(Saturated 2g)

Cholesterol 59mg

Fiber 10g

Sodium 183mg

Eggplant Parmesan

Yield:
6 servings

Serving Size:
4 ½ x 4 ⅓-inch piece

Preparation Time:
15–20 minutes

Cooking Time:
30 minutes

Nutrition Analysis Per Serving:

Calories 237

Protein 14g

Carbohydrate 27g

Fat 9g

(Saturated 4g)

Cholesterol 20mg

Fiber 2g

Sodium 933mg

1–3 T. flour
1 lb. eggplant
2 egg whites
2 T. skim milk
⅔ c. Italian breadcrumbs
Cooking spray
1 jar (26 oz.) your favorite spaghetti sauce
1 ½ c. (6 oz.) shredded part-skim mozzarella cheese
3 T. grated Parmesan cheese

Preheat oven to 400°. Place flour in a large sealable plastic bag; set aside. Peel and cut eggplant into ½-inch thick slices (approximately 12). Place slices in plastic bag; shake to coat. Combine egg whites and milk. Dip each eggplant slice into egg white mixture and lightly coat them on all sides with Italian breadcrumbs. Place slices on a baking sheet coated with cooking spray. Bake 12–15 minutes or until lightly browned and tender. Reduce oven temperature to 350°.

Lightly coat a 13 x 9 x 2-inch baking dish with cooking spray. Place half the eggplant slices in a single layer on the bottom of the dish. Spoon half the spaghetti sauce over the slices and sprinkle with half the mozzarella cheese. Repeat, adding a second layer with the remaining ingredients. Top with Parmesan cheese and bake uncovered 15 minutes, or until thoroughly heated.

Zucchini Couscous

Couscous is a quick and delicious way to serve a new grain to your family.

1 medium zucchini, chopped
2 T. chopped green onion
2 T. low-sodium soy sauce
2 T. white wine
1 clove garlic, minced
½ c. uncooked couscous
½ c. water
1 ½ tsp. margarine

Combine the zucchini, green onions, soy sauce, white wine, and garlic in a 2-quart microwave-safe dish and mix well. Microwave, covered, on medium for 2 minutes. Stir in the couscous, water, and margarine. Microwave, covered, on high for 3 minutes. Let stand, still covered, for 5 minutes before serving.

To boost your fiber intake, eat a variety of grains such as couscous, bulgur, or quinoa.

Yield:
4 servings

Serving Size:
½ cup

Preparation Time:
10 minutes

Cooking Time:
5 minutes

Nutrition Analysis Per Serving:

Calories 115

Protein 4g

Carbohydrate 20g

Fat 2g

(Saturated <1g)

Cholesterol 0mg

Fiber 2g

Sodium 274mg

Lemon Caper Orzo

This recipe is the perfect accompaniment for fish or poultry. Try serving it with our recipe for Salmon with Tarragon Sauce (p. 175)

Yield:
6 servings

Serving Size:
½ cup

Preparation Time:
5 minutes

Cooking Time:
10–12 minutes

1 c. orzo, uncooked
½ tsp. salt
¼ c. chopped fresh parsley
3 T. fresh lemon juice
2 T. capers, drained and rinsed
1 tsp. olive oil
½ tsp. freshly ground pepper

Cook orzo according to package directions; drain. Stir the parsley, lemon juice, capers, olive oil, and pepper into the orzo. Serve immediately.

Nutrition Analysis Per Serving:

Calories 114

Protein 4g

Carbohydrate 22g

Fat 1g

(Saturated <1g)

Cholesterol 0mg

Fiber 1g

Sodium 282mg

Although orzo is a type of pasta, many mistake it for rice because of its similarity in shape and size. Orzo has a softer texture than rice.

Fish & Seafood

Shrimp Jambalaya

Yield:
6 servings

Serving Size:
1 cup

Preparation Time:
10–15 minutes

Cooking Time:
35–40 minutes

2 c. cooked rice
1 medium onion, diced
½ green bell pepper, diced
½ c. sliced mushrooms
2 tsp. oil
2 cans (14 ½ oz. each) Cajun-style tomatoes
1 T. flour
½ tsp. garlic powder
½ tsp. dried thyme leaves
⅛ tsp. cayenne pepper
⅛ tsp. ground cloves
2 bay leaves
1 c. diced cooked ham
1 pkg. (6 oz.) frozen cooked shrimp

Cook rice according to package directions;
set aside. In a large pot, sauté onion,
green pepper, and mushrooms in oil. Add
tomatoes and stir. Sprinkle mixture with
flour; cook and stir for 4 minutes. Stir in
the next 5 ingredients; cook for 4 minutes.
Reduce to simmer. Stir in ham, shrimp, and
cooked rice. Simmer for 20 minutes. Stir
occasionally and add water if necessary.

*Fresh fish is best when it's cooked and
eaten the same day it's purchased. When
that isn't possible, store fish on ice in
the coldest part of the refrigerator.*

Nutrition Analysis Per Serving:

Calories 194

Protein 13g

Carbohydrate 29g

Fat 3g

(Saturated 1g)

Cholesterol 67mg

Fiber 3g

Sodium 820mg

Spicy Shrimp Boil with Rice

A unique shrimp dish cooked in a spicy broth.

½ c. lemon juice
¼ c. olive oil
¼ c. packed brown sugar
1 ½ T. Worcestershire sauce
2 tsp. Italian seasoning
2 cloves garlic, minced
1 tsp. pepper
¼–½ tsp. crushed red pepper flakes
1 tsp. dried rosemary leaves
1 c. brown rice
1 lb. raw shrimp, peeled and deveined

In large saucepan, mix all ingredients except rice and shrimp. Let mixture stand 1–2 hours before cooking to blend flavors. Meanwhile, cook rice according to package directions. Ten minutes before serving time, bring spice mixture to a boil; add shrimp and cook until shrimp are pink. Serve over rice.

New analyses demonstrate that cholesterol values for shellfish are far lower than previously thought. Shrimp, clams, scallops, and lobster are now considered good selections, particularly since they are naturally low in calories and fat.

Yield:
4 servings

Serving Size:
1 ½ cups

Preparation Time:
5 minutes

Standing Time:
1–2 hours

Cooking Time:
40–50 minutes

Nutrition Analysis Per Serving:

Calories 484

Protein 27g

Carbohydrate 55g

Fat 17g

(Saturated 2g)

Cholesterol 172mg

Fiber 2g

Sodium 271mg

Garlic Shrimp on a Bun

Great for a light lunch on the deck or patio.

Yield:
6 cups

Serving Size:
½ roll with 4 oz. shrimp

Preparation Time:
5–10 minutes

Cooking Time:
15 minutes

Cooking spray
¼ c. chopped green onion
2–3 cloves garlic, minced
2 tsp. olive oil
⅔ c. dry white wine
¼ c. lemon juice
⅛ tsp. salt
⅛ tsp. black pepper
1 tsp. dried dillweed
1 ½ lbs. medium-size raw shrimp, peeled and deveined
3 French rolls, split lengthwise and toasted

In a non-stick skillet coated with cooking spray, sauté onion and garlic in olive oil until tender; add wine, lemon juice, salt, pepper, and dill. Bring mixture to a boil and let simmer 5 minutes to blend flavors. Add shrimp and cook 3–5 minutes longer until shrimp are pink. Spoon over toasted rolls and serve immediately.

Nutrition Analysis Per Serving:

Calories 210

Protein 25g

Carbohydrate 12g

Fat 4g

(*Saturated 1g*)

Cholesterol 172mg

Fiber 1g

Sodium 383mg

Always purchase seafood and shellfish at reputable stores to ensure its quality and safety. Purchasing fish at roadside sales may be tempting, but your health could be at stake if the fish was harvested from unsafe waters.

Fettuccine with Shrimp Sauce

8 oz. spinach fettuccine noodles
1 ½ c. low-sodium chicken broth
¼ c. dry white wine
¼ tsp. dried whole marjoram
Dash of black pepper
¾ lb. fresh or frozen raw shrimp,
peeled and deveined
1 T. cornstarch
1 c. skim milk
2 slices (1 oz. each) reduced-fat Swiss
cheese, sliced into thin strips
2 T. snipped chives or green onion tops

Cook pasta according to package directions;
set aside. Meanwhile, combine chicken broth,
wine, marjoram, and pepper in a saucepan;
bring to a boil. Add shrimp and return
mixture to boiling. Cook 1 minute or until
shrimp are pink. Remove shrimp from sauce
into another dish; cover and set aside. Bring
broth mixture to a full boil; boil 20 minutes
or until sauce is reduced to ½ cup. Whisk
cornstarch and milk; add to reduced mixture
in saucepan. Cook sauce 2 minutes or until
thickened and bubbly. Add cheese and chives;
stir until cheese is melted. Return shrimp to
saucepan; heat through. Serve over pasta.

*The best test for seafood freshness is
the sniff test—if seafood smells strong,
"fishy," or like ammonia, don't buy it.*

Yield:
4 servings

Serving Size:
1 ½ cups

Preparation Time:
15 minutes

Cooking Time:
30–35 minutes

**Nutrition Analysis
Per Serving:**

Calories 402

Protein 34g

Carbohydrate 47g

Fat 7g

(Saturated 4g)

Cholesterol 143mg

Fiber 3g

Sodium 431mg

Clam-Filled Lasagna Rolls

Yield:
4 servings

Serving Size:
2 rolls

Preparation Time:
15–20 minutes

Cooking Time:
35–40 minutes

8 lasagna noodle strips
1 can (6 ½ oz.) chopped clams, reserve liquid
2 c. your favorite spaghetti sauce
1 container (15 oz.) light ricotta cheese
½ c. grated Parmesan cheese
1 egg, beaten
1 T. dried parsley flakes

Cook noodles according to package directions and drain. Preheat oven to 350°. Combine clam liquid and spaghetti sauce. Spoon half of the sauce into a 9 x 9-inch baking dish and spread until dish bottom is covered. In a medium bowl, combine clams, ricotta, Parmesan, egg, and parsley; mix well. Spread equal portions of clam and cheese mixture on entire length of lasagna noodles and roll up jellyroll fashion. Place, seam side down, in prepared baking dish. Top with remaining sauce; cover. Bake 35–45 minutes, or until hot.

Nutrition Analysis Per Serving:

Calories 485

Protein 34g

Carbohydrate 55g

Fat 13g

(Saturated 5g)

Cholesterol 118mg

Fiber 4g

Sodium 834mg

Most pasta is made from durum semolina. This type of wheat has a slightly higher protein content than wheat used in bread products.

Scallops with Peppers & Pasta

A beautiful green, red, and white presentation in a light sauce.

2 c. thin spinach pasta, uncooked
1 T. margarine
½ lb. bay scallops
1 large red bell pepper, sliced into strips
½ c. dry white wine
¼ c. lemon juice
1 clove garlic, minced

Cook pasta according to package directions. Melt margarine in a medium non-stick skillet; add scallops and red pepper; cook until scallops are opaque. Remove scallop and pepper mixture from pan; set aside. To skillet, add wine, lemon juice, and garlic; reduce to about half the original volume. Stir in pasta and scallop and pepper mixture. Heat and serve.

When buying scallops, look for firm, distinctive shapes. Scallops that appear to be melting into one another are past their prime.

Yield:
4 servings

Serving Size:
1 ½ cup

Preparation Time:
10 minutes

Cooking Time:
15 minutes

Nutrition Analysis Per Serving:

Calories 216

Protein 18g

Carbohydrate 21g

Fat 4g

(Saturated 1g)

Cholesterol 37mg

Fiber 3g

Sodium 218mg

Grilled Tuna Steaks

Yield:
4 servings

Serving Size:
5 ounces

Preparation Time:
5 minutes

Marinating Time:
1 hour

Cooking Time:
10 minutes

4 (5 oz. each) tuna steaks
½ c. lowfat Italian dressing
2 tsp. low-sodium soy sauce
2 tsp. lemon juice

Place tuna steaks in a 2-inch-deep dish. Combine Italian dressing, soy sauce, and lemon juice; pour over tuna steaks. Cover and refrigerate 1 hour, turning once. Remove steaks from marinade and reserve marinade. Grill tuna over medium coals for 5 minutes on each side or until fish flakes easily when tested with a fork. Baste occasionally with marinade.

Nutrition Analysis Per Serving:

Calories 214

Protein 33g

Carbohydrate 1g

Fat 8g

(Saturated 2g)

Cholesterol 54mg

Fiber <1g

Sodium 93mg

When handling raw poultry, meat, or fish, wash your hands, the counters, utensils, and cutting boards with hot soapy water between recipe steps. Never put cooked poultry, meat, or fish on the plate that held it when it was uncooked, unless the plate has since been washed.

Grilled Tuna with Strawberry Salsa

Serve this with our Fire-Grilled Vegetables (p. 109) for a satisfying meal.

Strawberry Salsa:
1 pint fresh strawberries, hulled and coarsely chopped
4 green onions, chopped
2 tsp. Dijon mustard
1 tsp. orange zest
1 tsp. red wine vinegar

Tuna:
4 (6 oz.) tuna steaks
1 tsp. canola oil
Salt and black pepper, to taste

Yield:
4 servings

Serving Size:
1 steak with ¼ of salsa

Preparation Time:
5 minutes

Cooking Time:
10 minutes

For the salsa, combine the strawberries, green onions, Dijon mustard, orange zest, and wine vinegar in a bowl and mix gently. Cover and chill for 1 hour. For the tuna, brush each side of the steaks lightly with canola oil. Sprinkle with salt and pepper. Grill over medium-hot coals for 10 minutes or until the tuna flakes easily, turning once. Remove the tuna to a serving platter. Top each steak with ¼ of the salsa just before serving.

When we think salsa, we typically think tomato. However, salsa can be made from a variety of fruit or vegetables. Salsas are so refreshing they enhance even the blandest of foods.

Nutrition Analysis Per Serving:

Calories 290

Protein 42g

Carbohydrate 6g

Fat 10g

(Saturated 2g)

Cholesterol 67mg

Fiber 2g

Sodium 134mg

Teriyaki Halibut

This teriyaki marinade is flavorful, and has no oil.

Yield:
4 servings

Serving Size:
6 ounces

Preparation Time:
5 minutes

Marinating Time:
2 hours

Cooking Time:
15–35 minutes

Nutrition Analysis Per Serving:

Calories 243

Protein 37g

Carbohydrate 2g

Fat 4g

(Saturated 1g)

Cholesterol 54mg

Fiber <1g

Sodium 488mg

1 c. white or rosé wine
¼ c. low-sodium soy sauce
2 cloves garlic, minced
2 tsp. ground ginger
1 tsp. dried oregano leaves
Black pepper, to taste
4 (6 oz. each) halibut steaks

Combine first 6 ingredients and pour over halibut steaks. Cover and marinate several hours or overnight in the refrigerator. Grill halibut about 10–15 minutes, depending on the thickness of the steaks, basting occasionally with marinade; or bake for 30–35 minutes in marinade. Remove from marinade and serve.

Halibut in Red Pepper Sauce

This tremendous sauce is worth the extra effort.

2 large red bell peppers
1 tsp. olive oil
½ c. diced onion
2 cloves garlic, minced
½ tsp. dried oregano leaves, or
1 ½ tsp. fresh oregano
1 T. vinegar
¼–½ c. low-sodium chicken broth
4 (6 oz. each) halibut steaks
Salt and black pepper, to taste

Broil peppers on top rack of oven, turning until evenly cooked (peppers are done when they blister). Place peppers in a small paper bag and let cool 15–20 minutes; remove from bag, peel, and seed. Cut peppers into chunks. Heat oil in a non-stick skillet over medium heat. Add onion and garlic; sauté until tender. Place onion mixture, roasted pepper chunks, oregano, and vinegar in blender. Add 2 tablespoons broth and process; continue to add broth until desired consistency.

Bring about 2 inches of water to boil in a large Dutch oven. Salt and pepper halibut steaks; place steaks in a vegetable steamer and place steamer in Dutch oven. Cover and steam 12–15 minutes or until fish flakes easily when tested with a fork. Serve with red pepper sauce.

Fish marked "fresh" means that it has never been frozen—not that it was caught just hours ago.

Yield:
4 servings

Serving Size:
6 ounces

Preparation Time:
25 minutes

Cooking Time:
15 minutes

Nutrition Analysis Per Serving:

Calories 233

Protein 37g

Carbohydrate 8g

Fat 5g

(Saturated 1g)

Cholesterol 55mg

Fiber 2g

Sodium 169mg

Honey-Mustard Salmon

Yield:
2 servings

Serving Size:
5 ounces

Preparation Time:
5–10 minutes

Marinating Time:
2–4 hours

Cooking Time:
10–15 minutes

2 T. rum
4 tsp. Dijon mustard
1 T. honey
1 T. lemon juice
¼ tsp. black pepper
2 (5 oz. each) salmon steaks

In a small mixing bowl, whisk together the first 5 ingredients. Brush both sides of each salmon steak with marinade. Cover and refrigerate several hours. Grill fish over medium-hot coals, turning once, until steaks flake easily when tested with a fork. Alternatively, you can broil 6 inches from heat 6–8 minutes or until done.

Nutrition Analysis Per Serving:

Calories 335

Protein 28g

Carbohydrate 9g

Fat 15g

(Saturated 3g)

Cholesterol 84mg

Fiber <1g

Sodium 214mg

Salmon with Tarragon Sauce

So elegant, they'll think you've been cooking all day. (But we know how truly simple this recipe really is!)

4 (6 oz. each) salmon steaks
Cooking spray
½ c. dry white wine
1 ½ tsp. dried tarragon, divided
1 c. plain nonfat or lowfat yogurt
3 T. Dijon mustard
Lemon slices
Fresh parsley

Preheat oven to 350°. Rinse salmon; pat dry. Place salmon in baking dish coated with cooking spray. Pour wine over fish; sprinkle with ½ tsp. dried tarragon. Bake fish for 10–15 minutes or until salmon flakes easily when tested with a fork. Meanwhile, in medium saucepan, slowly warm yogurt, mustard, and 1 tsp. tarragon, stirring occasionally. Divide sauce among 4 heated plates. Place salmon on top of sauce and garnish with lemon slices and fresh parsley.

If by mistake a dish made with yogurt boils and curdles, it's still okay to eat—the appearance is just not as pleasing.

Yield:
4 servings

Serving Size:
6 ounces

Preparation Time:
5 minutes

Cooking Time:
10–15 minutes

Nutrition Analysis Per Serving:

Calories 300

Protein 39g

Carbohydrate 8g

Fat 11g

(Saturated 2g)

Cholesterol 95mg

Fiber <1g

Sodium 380mg

Linguine with Salmon & Lemon Sauce

For an easy end to a hectic day—keep ingredients for this quick meal in your pantry.

Yield:
4 servings

Serving Size:
1 ¼ cups

Preparation Time:
10 minutes

Cooking Time:
15 minutes

8 oz. spinach linguine noodles, uncooked
2 T. olive oil
½ c. diced onion
2 cloves garlic, minced
½ tsp. grated lemon peel
⅓ c. lemon juice
2 T. chopped fresh parsley
1 can (7 ¾ oz.) salmon, drained,
or cooked salmon
2 T. grated Parmesan cheese

Cook pasta according to package directions. While pasta is cooking, prepare sauce. Heat oil in a large skillet over low heat; add onion and sauté until tender. Add garlic; sauté another 2 minutes. Stir in lemon peel, lemon juice, and parsley. Add salmon and carefully break up meat with a fork. Do not stir. Toss linguine and sauce together. Sprinkle with Parmesan cheese and serve immediately.

Nutrition Analysis Per Serving:

Calories 371

Protein 21g

Carbohydrate 47g

Fat 11g

(Saturated 2g)

Cholesterol 24mg

Fiber 2g

Sodium 311mg

Lemon zest, the yellow-colored part of the lemon rind, is often used in recipes since a small quantity of lemon zest can add a much stronger lemon flavor than lemon juice alone.

Easy Salmon Cakes

Including more fish in your diet was never so easy.

1 can (15.5 oz.) pink salmon, drained
1 whole egg or 2 egg whites
½ c. crushed cornflake cereal
¼ c. minced onion
2 T. lemon juice
1 T. oil

Mash salmon with fork. Add egg, or egg whites, crushed cereal, onion, and lemon juice. Mix thoroughly; form 4 cakes. Heat oil over medium heat in a non-stick skillet. Add cakes and cook 6–8 minutes or until browned; turn and cook 4–6 more minutes or until browned.

Tip: Try serving with *Tarragon Sauce* (p. 175), *Creamy Dill Sauce* (p. 178), or *Cucumber-Dill Sauce* (p. 183)

Canned fish such as salmon and sardines can be a good source of calcium because the bones are never removed before canning.

Yield:
4 servings

Serving Size:
4-ounce cake

Preparation Time:
5 minutes

Cooking Time:
10–15 minutes

Nutrition Analysis Per Serving:

Calories 217

Protein 20g

Carbohydrate 5g

Fat 13g

(Saturated 2g)

Cholesterol 78mg

Fiber <1g

Sodium 126mg

Cod in Creamy Dill Sauce

Marvelous—and low calorie too!

Yield:
4 servings

Serving Size:
5 ounces

Preparation Time:
3–5 minutes

Cooking Time:
10 minutes

1 c. plain nonfat or lowfat yogurt
2 T. Dijon mustard
1 tsp. dried dillweed
1 ½ lb. Cod fillets

Combine yogurt, mustard, and dill; set aside 20 minutes to allow flavors to blend. Steam, broil, or grill fish until it flakes easily when tested with a fork. Spoon dill sauce over fish and serve.

Nutrition Analysis Per Serving:

Calories 188

Protein 36g

Carbohydrate 6g

Fat 2g

(Saturated <1g)

Cholesterol 83mg

Fiber <1g

Sodium 352mg

The "10-Minute Rule of Fish Cookery" applies anytime you are grilling, broiling, poaching, or sautéing fish. Measure the fish at its thickest point; then cook the fish for about 10 minutes per inch of thickness (turning it halfway through the cooking time).

Chinese-Style Poached Fish

3 c. water
6 fish fillets (cod, sole, or other
white fish, about 6 oz. each)
½ c. chopped green onion
¼ c. low-sodium soy sauce
3 T. rice vinegar
1 T. sesame oil
3 T. grated fresh ginger root
2–3 T. water
Black pepper, to taste

Bring water to boil in a large skillet. Place
fish fillets in the boiling water, cover, and
reduce heat to a simmer. Poach fish about
5–7 minutes, or until fish flakes easily when
tested with a fork. While fish is cooking,
heat onions, soy sauce, rice vinegar, sesame
oil, ginger, water, and pepper in a small
saucepan. Remove fish from water with a
slotted spoon and transfer to a plate. Spoon
ginger sauce over fish and serve immediately.

Yield:
6 servings

Serving Size:
1 fillet
1 tablespoon sauce

Preparation Time:
10 minutes

Cooking Time:
10 minutes

**Nutrition Analysis
Per Serving:**

Calories 186

Protein 34g

Carbohydrate 2g

Fat 4g

(Saturated <1g)

Cholesterol 69mg

Fiber <1g

Sodium 384mg

Italian Fish in Foil

A great make-ahead meal for company. Simply remove the prepared foil packets from your refrigerator and slip them on the grill

Yield:
4 servings

Serving Size:
6 ounces

Preparation Time:
15–20 minutes

Cooking Time:
20 minutes

Cooking spray
2 T. chopped green onions
¾ c. dry white wine
½ c. sliced fresh mushrooms
1 T. cornstarch
⅓ c. water
1 can (16 oz.) Italian-style tomatoes with basil, drained
2 T. lemon juice
2 T. fresh parsley, minced
½ tsp. black pepper
¼ tsp. salt
1 lb. sole (or cod) fillets
1 c. fresh or frozen raw shrimp, peeled and deveined

Nutrition Analysis Per Serving:

Calories 217

Protein 32g

Carbohydrate 8g

Fat 2g

(Saturated <1g)

Cholesterol 107mg

Fiber 1g

Sodium 509mg

Lightly coat a medium non-stick skillet with cooking spray. Add onions and sauté over medium heat until tender; stir in wine and mushrooms and continue to cook until mushrooms are tender. Whisk cornstarch with ⅓ cup water until smooth; stir into mushroom mix. Cook, stirring constantly, until mixture boils and thickens. Continue to cook and stir for 1 minute; stir in tomatoes, lemon juice, parsley, pepper, and salt. Place equal portions of fish on each of 4 pieces of heavy-duty aluminum foil. Divide the shrimp and tomato sauce mixture equally among the portions of fish. Seal fish in foil and place on grill 4–6 inches from medium-hot coals. Cook for 15 minutes on grill or bake in 400° oven for about 15–20 minutes or until fish flakes easily when tested with a fork.

Fish Olé

Fish takes on a new twist when baked with a Mexican flair.

1 ½ lb. white fish (pollock, snapper, cod fillets)
Cooking spray
1 c. your favorite salsa
4 oz. shredded reduced-fat Monterey Jack cheese

Preheat oven to 350°. Wash fillets and pat dry. Place fillets in a 13 x 9 x 2-inch glass casserole dish lightly coated with cooking spray; pour salsa over fish. Sprinkle with shredded cheese. Bake 20–25 minutes or until fish flakes easily when tested with a fork.

Yield:
4 servings

Serving Size:
5 ounces

Preparation Time:
5 minutes

Cooking Time:
20–25 minutes

Nutrition Analysis Per Serving:

Calories 239

Protein 37g

Carbohydrate 5g

Fat 7g

(Saturated 4g)

Cholesterol 83mg

Fiber 0g

Sodium 591mg

Many studies have found that as few as two fish meals per week may reduce the risk of heart disease. The benefits of fish are partially due to Omega-3 fatty acids, a polyunsaturated fat that may make artery walls less prone to blood clot formation.

Fish Tacos

You will be surprised how easy these delicious tacos are to prepare.

Yield:
8 servings

Serving Size:
1 taco

Preparation Time:
10 minutes

Cilantro Sauce:
½ c. lowfat ranch salad dressing
½ c. plain nonfat or lowfat yogurt
½ c. trimmed fresh cilantro leaves
2 T. chopped canned green chiles

Tacos:
1 lb. any type of white fish, grilled
2 c. shredded cabbage
1 avocado, cut into 8 slices
8 (6-inch) flour tortillas
Juice of 1 lime

For the sauce, combine the salad dressing, yogurt, cilantro, and chiles in a blender or food processor. Process until smooth. For the tacos, cut the fish into eight 2-oz. portions. Layer ¼ c. cabbage, 2 oz. fish, and 1 slice avocado on each tortilla. Fold over to enclose filling. Top each taco with some of the sauce and drizzle with lime juice.

Tip: If time is of the essence, substitute frozen grilled fish fillets for the grilled white fish and coleslaw mix for the shredded cabbage.

When poaching fish, add lemon juice to the water to ensure that the fish retains that bright white color.

Nutrition Analysis Per Serving:

Calories 341

Protein 19g

Carbohydrate 31g

Fat 15g

(Saturated 3g)

Cholesterol 46mg

Fiber 3g

Sodium 403mg

Trout with Cucumber-Dill Sauce

When you're lucky enough to have fresh trout, use this grilling idea at home or over a campfire.

4 whole pan-sized trout, cleaned
1 lemon, sliced
2 tsp. canola oil

Cucumber-Dill Sauce:
1 c. plain nonfat or lowfat yogurt
¼ c. light mayonnaise
1 c. peeled grated cucumber, drained
1 tsp. dried dillweed
½ tsp. lemon juice
½ tsp. black pepper

Insert several slices of lemon into the cavity of each trout; brush the outside of each fish with oil. Grill over high heat for 5–7 minutes per side, or until fish flakes easily when tested with a fork. Serve whole trout with extra lemon wedges.

Sauce:
Combine yogurt and mayonnaise, stirring until smooth. Stir in remaining ingredients.

Hint: Cucumber-Dill Sauce goes well with any kind of fish, seafood, or poultry, and as a dip with vegetables or crackers.

Yield:
4 servings

Serving Size:
1 trout

Preparation Time:
5 minutes

Cooking Time:
10–14 minutes

Nutrition Analysis Per Serving:

Calories 186

Protein 18g

Carbohydrate 7g

Fat 10g

(Saturated 2g)

Cholesterol 51mg

Fiber <1g

Sodium 32mg

Trout Almandine

A special way to prepare your freshly-caught trout.

Yield:
4 servings

Serving Size:
1 fillet

Preparation Time:
8 minutes

Cooking Time:
15–20 minutes

¼ c. cornmeal
¼ c. flour
¼ tsp. salt
¼ tsp. black pepper
4 trout fillets
½ c. skim milk
Cooking spray
1 tsp. margarine
3 T. slivered almonds
2 T. white wine
4 lemon wedges

Preheat oven to 400°. Combine cornmeal, flour, salt, and pepper. Dip fillets in skim milk; then coat with cornmeal mixture. Coat a baking rack (a cake cooling rack works well) with cooking spray; place rack in a jellyroll pan. Place trout fillets on rack and bake for 15–20 minutes or until fish flakes easily when tested with a fork.

Meanwhile, heat margarine in non-stick skillet, on medium heat. Sauté almonds in margarine; add wine. Pour evenly over cooked fish. Serve with a lemon wedge.

Oilier cold-water fish such as trout, salmon, mackerel, herring, sardines, fresh tuna, and halibut contain the Omega-3 fatty acids that have been shown to help prevent heart disease.

Nutrition Analysis Per Serving:

Calories 225

Protein 20g

Carbohydrate 17g

Fat 8g

(Saturated 2g)

Cholesterol 47mg

Fiber 2g

Sodium 202mg

Poultry

Sesame-Ginger Chicken

Yield:
4 servings

Serving Size:
1 chicken breast half

Preparation Time:
10 minutes

Marinating Time:
4 hours

Cooking Time:
10–15 minutes

4 boneless, skinless chicken breast halves
¼ c. low-sodium soy sauce
2 T. water
1 T. dried onion flakes
1 T. sesame seeds
½ tsp. ground ginger
1 clove garlic, minced

Place chicken in a bowl or plastic bag. Combine soy sauce and remaining ingredients; pour over chicken. Cover or seal and marinate in the refrigerator 4 hours or longer, turning occasionally. Remove chicken from marinade. Grill over medium-high heat for 5 minutes; turn and continue cooking until done.

Nutrition Analysis Per Serving:

Calories 150

Protein 28g

Carbohydrate 2g

Fat 3g

(Saturated <1g)

Cholesterol 68mg

Fiber <1g

Sodium 180mg

Less marinade is needed if you marinate meats by placing them in a tightly sealed plastic bag with its excess air squeezed out.

Sweet & Sour Chicken

1 c. brown rice, uncooked
¾ lb. boneless, skinless
chicken breasts, cubed
1 T. peanut oil
1 c. sliced carrots
1 clove garlic, minced
1 c. green bell pepper strips
1 can (8 oz.) pineapple chunks, in juice
1 T. cornstarch
¼ c. low-sodium soy sauce
3 T. brown sugar
3 T. vinegar
½ tsp. ground ginger

Yield:
4 servings

Serving Size:
1 ⅔ cups

Preparation Time:
20 minutes

Cooking Time:
20 minutes

Cook rice according to package directions. In a large skillet, brown chicken in peanut oil. Add carrots and garlic; stir and cook 1–2 minutes. Add green pepper and pineapple with juice. Combine cornstarch, soy sauce, sugar, vinegar, and ginger; add to chicken mixture. Bring to a boil, stirring constantly until sauce thickens. Serve over hot rice.

Peanut oil is the oil of choice for stir-frying. It can be heated to extremely high temperatures before it begins to smoke.

Nutrition Analysis Per Serving:

Calories 401

Protein 23g

Carbohydrate 61g

Fat 7g

(Saturated 1g)

Cholesterol 47mg

Fiber 4g

Sodium 467mg

Broccoli-Cashew Chicken

Yield:
4 servings

Serving Size:
1 ⅓ cups

Preparation Time:
15 minutes

Cooking Time:
10–15 minutes

2 T. low-sodium soy sauce
2 tsp. cooking sherry
1 ½ tsp. sugar
1 ½ tsp. white wine vinegar
1 tsp. cornstarch
Dash hot pepper sauce
1 T. low-sodium soy sauce
1 tsp. cornstarch
4 boneless, skinless chicken breast halves, cubed
1 T. peanut oil, divided
½ c. cashew nuts
2 c. broccoli florets
1 medium onion, cut in 8 wedges
2 cloves garlic, minced
¼ tsp. ground ginger

Nutrition Analysis Per Serving:

Calories 307

Protein 32g

Carbohydrate 16g

Fat 13g

(*Saturated 3g*)

Cholesterol 68mg

Fiber 2g

Sodium 298mg

Combine first 6 ingredients; set aside. Whisk 1 tablespoon soy sauce and 1 teaspoon cornstarch in a medium bowl. Add chicken cubes and stir to coat; set aside. Over medium heat, heat half of the oil in wok. Add cashews and stir-fry until brown (about 1 minute). Remove nuts; set aside. Add remaining oil to wok. When oil is hot, add chicken and stir-fry 2–3 minutes until chicken starts to turn opaque. Add broccoli, onion, garlic, and ginger; continue to stir until broccoli becomes tender. Add reserved sauce and stir-fry until sauce thickens. Add nuts, stir, and serve.

Stir-fry meals are a good way of disguising smaller meat portions; colorful vegetables make up the bulk of your stir-fry meal.

Chicken in Peanut Sauce

This Indonesian recipe has an unusual combination of textures that gets delightful results.

¼ c. chunky peanut butter
3 T. low-sodium soy sauce
2 T. red wine vinegar
2 T. water
2 tsp. sesame oil
½ tsp. crushed red pepper flakes
1 T. peanut oil
1 lb chicken, cut into 1 ½-inch strips
1 clove garlic, minced
1 c. sliced green bell pepper
1 c. julienne cut zucchini
1 c. julienne cut carrots
8 oz. angel hair pasta
2 c. shredded leaf lettuce (optional)

In a small bowl combine peanut butter, soy sauce, vinegar, water, sesame oil, and red pepper flakes. Stir until mixture is well blended; set aside. Heat peanut oil in wok. Add chicken and garlic; stir-fry for 4–5 minutes. Push chicken up the sides of the wok and add green pepper, zucchini, and carrots. Stir-fry until the vegetables are crisp yet tender (about 3 minutes). Meanwhile, cook pasta according to package directions to just *al dente*. Toss pasta with peanut sauce. To serve, arrange cooked pasta in a peanut sauce on plate and top with shredded lettuce (if desired). Spoon chicken and vegetable mixture on top.

Yield:
4 servings

Serving Size:
1 ⅔ cups

Preparation Time:
20 minutes

Cooking Time:
10 minutes

Nutrition Analysis Per Serving:

Calories 430

Protein 34g

Carbohydrate 34g

Fat 18g

(Saturated 3g)

Cholesterol 66mg

Fiber 5g

Sodium 604mg

Blackened Chicken Breasts

Use this spice mix on chicken, fish, and lean beef for a snappy entrée.

Yield:
4 servings

Serving Size:
1 chicken breast half

Preparation Time:
5 minutes

Cooking Time:
15–18 minutes

1 T. paprika
1 tsp. onion powder
1 tsp. garlic powder
1 tsp. cayenne pepper
¾ tsp. white pepper
¾ tsp. black pepper
½ tsp. salt
½ tsp. dried thyme leaves
½ tsp. dried oregano leaves
4 boneless, skinless chicken breast halves
1 T. oil

Combine first 9 ingredients to make the blackened spice mix. Coat each chicken breast with about 1 teaspoon of the spice mix. Store remaining spice mix for another use. In a large non-stick skillet, cook chicken in hot oil over medium heat. Turn chicken over when first side is browned (about 7 minutes), and cook until done. You might also try serving this on a Kaiser roll with your favorite sandwich toppings.

Nutrition Analysis Per Serving:

Calories 173

Protein 28g

Carbohydrate 3g

Fat 5g

(Saturated 1g)

Cholesterol 68mg

Fiber 1g

Sodium 369mg

You were not born with a preference for salt—you learned it! This means that you can "unlearn" it by gradually lowering the amount of salt in your diet. Most people who do this lose their desire for the salty taste.

Wine-Poached Chicken

*White wine and tarragon delicately flavor this dish,
while fresh mushrooms lend a smooth texture.*

4 boneless, skinless chicken breast halves
⅓ lb. fresh mushrooms, sliced
½ tsp. salt
½ tsp. dried tarragon leaves
¼ tsp. pepper
2 T. fresh parsley, chopped
¾ c. dry white wine

Place chicken and mushrooms in a large
skillet; sprinkle with salt, tarragon, pepper,
and parsley. Pour wine over chicken. Cover
and simmer for 15 minutes or until chicken
is tender. Serve with sauce left from skillet.

Hint: For a delicious meal, serve this
dish with Awesome Asparagus (p.
104) and Garlic Mashers (p. 120).

*Taking the skin off a half breast of roasted
chicken reduces the fat from 8 grams to 3
grams, and calories from 195 to 140.*

Yield:
4 servings

Serving Size:
1 chicken breast half
with ¼ of sauce

Preparation Time:
10 minutes

Cooking Time:
15–20 minutes

**Nutrition Analysis
Per Serving:**

Calories 170

Protein 29g

Carbohydrate 2g

Fat 2g

(Saturated <1g)

Cholesterol 68mg

Fiber 1g

Sodium 372mg

Dijon Chicken

This recipe pays homage to a popular entrée at the Wellshire Inn restaurant.

Yield:
2 servings

Serving Size:
1 chicken breast half

Preparation Time:
7 minutes

Cooking Time:
10 minutes

½ c. white wine
2 shallots, finely diced
1 tsp. dried whole tarragon
1 T. Dijon mustard
1 T. honey
Salt and black pepper, to taste
2 boneless, skinless chicken breast halves

In a small saucepan, heat the white wine, shallots, and tarragon, uncovered, over medium-low heat until the sauce reduces by half. Remove from heat and stir in mustard, honey, salt, and pepper. Coat chicken with honey-mustard sauce and grill for 5 minutes. Turn chicken and baste with more sauce; cook until done. Serve with extra sauce on the side.

Nutrition Analysis Per Serving:

Calories 216

Protein 28g

Carbohydrate 12g

Fat 2g

(Saturated <1g)

Cholesterol 68mg

Fiber <1g

Sodium 180mg

Use a separate cutting board for raw meats. Clean utensils and boards in hot soapy water to prevent harmful bacteria from spreading.

Rosemary-Lemon Chicken

1 ½ c. sliced fresh mushrooms
1 clove garlic, minced
1 T. olive oil
2 T. flour
½ tsp. dried rosemary leaves
4 boneless, skinless chicken breast halves
¼ c. lemon juice
¼ c. chicken broth
2 T. chopped, fresh parsley

In a large non-stick skillet, sauté mushrooms and garlic in oil for 3–5 minutes. Remove from pan. Combine flour and rosemary; dust chicken with flour mixture and brown on both sides. Add lemon juice and broth to chicken and stir, scraping up any browned bits. Return mushrooms to pan. Cover and simmer for 15 minutes. Garnish with parsley.

Yield:
4 servings

Serving Size:
1 chicken breast half
with ¼ of sauce

Preparation Time:
20 minutes

Cooking Time:
20 minutes

**Nutrition Analysis
Per Serving:**

Calories 266

Protein 22g

Carbohydrate 6g

Fat 18g

(Saturated 5g)

Cholesterol 73mg

Fiber 1g

Sodium 70mg

Easy Italian Baked Chicken

Yield:
4 servings

Serving Size:
¼ of chicken

Preparation Time:
15 minutes

Marinating Time:
8 hours

Cooking Time:
1 hour

Nutrition Analysis Per Serving:

Calories 315

Protein 54g

Carbohydrate 13g

Fat 4g

(*Saturated 1g*)

Cholesterol 132mg

Fiber 1g

Sodium 663mg

½ c. lemon juice
1 c. lowfat Italian dressing
2 lbs. chicken, skinned and
cut into 1-inch cubes
1 ½ c. Italian breadcrumbs
½ tsp. salt
Cooking spray

Mix lemon juice and salad dressing together. Marinate chicken in lemon juice mixture in the refrigerator for at least 8 hours, or overnight, turning occasionally. Heat oven to 350°. Mix breadcrumbs and salt. Coat chicken pieces with crumbs and place on foil-covered cookie sheet coated with cooking spray. Bake 1 hour or until tender. Try this served over pasta or dipped in your favorite spaghetti sauce.

Tandoori Chicken

Served cold, this makes an elegant picnic for a concert in the park.

1 c. plain nonfat or lowfat yogurt
1 T. fresh lemon juice
1 T. low-sodium soy sauce
1 T. coriander
¼ tsp. curry powder
⅛ tsp. black pepper
4 bone-in chicken breast halves, skinned

Combine yogurt, lemon juice, soy sauce, coriander, curry powder, and pepper. Pour ¾ cup of yogurt mixture into a 1 ½-quart shallow baking dish. Cover and refrigerate remaining marinade. Place chicken breasts in baking dish, turning to coat all sides with sauce. Cover and marinate chicken in refrigerator several hours or overnight. Bake chicken, uncovered, at 375° for 40–45 minutes or until tender, basting frequently with reserved marinade.

Store spices in a cool place away from any direct source of heat. Heat will destroy their flavors. Red spices will maintain flavor and color longer if refrigerated.

Yield:
4 servings

Serving Size:
1 chicken breast half

Preparation Time:
10 minutes

Marinating Time:
2–12 hours

Cooking Time:
40–45 minutes

Nutrition Analysis Per Serving:

Calories 158

Protein 30g

Carbohydrate 6g

Fat 1g

(Saturated <1g)

Cholesterol 70mg

Fiber <1g

Sodium 232mg

Chicken Curry

If you like curry—you'll love this.

Yield:
4 servings

Serving Size:
¼ of chicken and
sauce

Preparation Time:
10 minutes

Cooking Time:
45 minutes

**Nutrition Analysis
Per Serving:**

Calories 368

Protein 53g

Carbohydrate 15g

Fat 10g

(Saturated 2g)

Cholesterol 159mg

Fiber 3g

Sodium 399mg

1 T. margarine
1 medium onion, diced
1 T. curry powder
1 tsp. ground ginger
¼ tsp. allspice
¼ tsp. cayenne pepper
¼ tsp. salt
¼ tsp. black pepper
1 can (6 oz.) tomato paste
½ c. plain nonfat or lowfat yogurt
2 lbs. chicken pieces, skinned
1 c. chicken broth (optional)

In a large non-stick skillet, melt margarine
and sauté onion; add spices and tomato
paste. Add yogurt gradually, stirring in
small spoonfuls at a time, to avoid curdling.
Stir until sauce is smooth. Add chicken
pieces, spooning sauce over chicken to coat;
cover and simmer about 45 minutes or until
chicken is tender. (This recipe makes a dry
type of chicken. If a sauce is desired, add
1 cup chicken broth during simmering.)

Moroccan-Style Chicken Breasts

½ c. bulgur or cracked wheat
¼ c. diced onion
¼ c. shredded carrot
¼ c. thinly sliced celery
1 c. low-sodium chicken broth
4 boneless, skinless chicken breast halves
1 T. canola oil

Sauce:
½ c. dry white wine
½ c. low-sodium chicken broth
1 T. chopped fresh parsley

Yield:
4 servings

Serving Size:
1 chicken breast
with ½ cup bulgur

Preparation Time:
20–25 minutes

Cooking Time:
25 minutes

In a saucepan, combine bulgur, onion, carrot, celery, and broth. Bring to a boil. Reduce heat; cover and simmer 15 minutes or until bulgur is done. Cut a pocket in the thickest part of each breast half. Spoon bulgur mixture into each pocket; reserve remaining mixture. Secure pockets with wooden picks. In a large non-stick skillet, cook chicken in oil over medium heat. Turn chicken once during cooking. Cook about 10–15 minutes or until done. Remove picks; place chicken in a shallow serving dish. Sprinkle remaining bulgur mixture over chicken and keep warm. To skillet, add wine and chicken broth. Boil uncovered about 5 minutes or until reduced to ½ cup. Spoon sauce over chicken breasts and garnish with parsley.

**Nutrition Analysis
Per Serving:**

Calories 263

Protein 31g

Carbohydrate 17g

Fat 6g

(Saturated 1g)

Cholesterol 68mg

Fiber 4g

Sodium 120mg

Mediterranean Chicken

Yield:
4 servings

Serving Size:
¼ of chicken and
vegetables

Preparation Time:
15–20 minutes

Cooking Time:
50–60 minutes

**Nutrition Analysis
Per Serving:**

Calories 371

Protein 56g

Carbohydrate 19g

Fat 8g

(Saturated 2g)

Cholesterol 159mg

Fiber 5g

Sodium 964mg

Cooking spray
2 lbs. chicken, skinned and cubed
1 tsp. salt, divided
¼ tsp. black pepper
1 can (14 ½ oz.) diced tomatoes, undrained
½ c. diced onion
1 clove garlic, minced
2 tsp. dried basil leaves
1 bay leaf
3 medium zucchini, cut into 2-inch strips
1 green bell pepper, cut into strips
1 lb. fresh mushrooms, halved
2 T. flour
Parmesan cheese, grated (optional)

Preheat oven to 425°. Coat a 13 x 9 x 2-inch metal baking pan with cooking spray. Add chicken and sprinkle with ½ teaspoon salt and the pepper. Bake 10 minutes. Reduce oven temperature to 350°. In a large bowl, combine tomatoes, onions, garlic, basil, bay leaf, zucchini, green pepper, mushrooms, and remaining ½ tsp. salt; stir well. Pour mixture over chicken; cover and bake about 40–50 minutes more or until tender. Remove chicken from pan; set aside. Remove ½ cup of liquid from baking pan; stir in flour until smooth. Add the liquid back to vegetables in pan and cook over medium heat until sauce thickens. Pour vegetable sauce over chicken and sprinkle with Parmesan cheese, if desired.

Cortez Chicken Enchiladas

This is a delectable variation of the Mexican enchilada, and goes well with our recipe for Mexican Cornbread (p. 135).

½ c. chopped onion
½ c. chopped green bell pepper
1 can (4 oz.) chopped green chiles
½ c. chicken broth
2 c. canned green chili
enchilada sauce, divided
½ T. chili powder
1 tsp. black pepper
2 cloves garlic, minced
1 lb. cooked chicken breast, shredded, or 15 oz. canned chunk chicken in water, drained
12 corn tortillas
Cooking spray
1 c. shredded, part-skim mozzarella cheese

Yield:
6 servings

Serving Size:
2 enchiladas

Preparation Time:
25 minutes

Cooking Time:
20 minutes

Preheat oven to 375°. Combine onion, green pepper, green chiles, chicken broth, and ⅓ cup of enchilada sauce in a large non-stick skillet; cook for 5 minutes. Add chili powder, pepper, garlic, and chicken. Mix well; cover and simmer for 5 minutes or until thoroughly heated.

Meanwhile, heat corn tortillas by wrapping them in paper towels and microwaving on high for 1 ½–2 minutes. Spread ⅓ c. of chicken mixture lengthwise on each tortilla. Roll tortilla and place, seam side down, in a shallow baking dish coated with cooking spray; pour remaining enchilada sauce over and sprinkle with cheese. Bake for 20 minutes or until thoroughly heated.

Nutrition Analysis Per Serving:

Calories 401

Protein 32g

Carbohydrate 37g

Fat 13g

(*Saturated 6g*)

Cholesterol 89mg

Fiber 5g

Sodium 345mg

Game Hens in Orange Sauce

Ginger and cinnamon add a subtle spice and fragrant aroma to this special-occasion dish. Serve these game hens with couscous or Savory Green Rice (p. 156) for an elegant meal.

Yield:
4 servings

Serving Size:
½ of hen and sauce

Preparation Time:
15–20 minutes

Cooking Time:
55–65 minutes

2 each Cornish hens, cut in half
½ t. salt
3 T. canola oil
3 T. flour
¼ t. cinnamon
⅛ t. ginger
¼ t. salt
1 ½ c. orange juice
¼ c. water, if needed
¼ c. almonds, sliced
⅓ c. raisins

Nutrition Analysis Per Serving:

Calories 365

Protein 27g

Carbohydrate 25g

Fat 18g

(Saturated 2g)

Cholesterol 109mg

Fiber 2g

Sodium 520mg

Preheat oven to 375°. Remove skin from Cornish hen halves; rinse and pat dry. Season hen halves with ½ teaspoon salt and place in shallow baking dish. Cover loosely with foil and place in preheated oven; roast for 30 minutes. While hens are cooking, heat oil in a sauce pan; combine flour, cinnamon, ginger, and ¼ teaspoon salt; add to heated oil to make a smooth paste. Cook 1–2 minutes, or until slightly browned. Slowly whisk in orange juice; cook over medium heat, stirring constantly, until mixture is thickened and bubbly. Remove from heat; stir in almonds and raisins.

At the end of 30 minutes, remove foil from hens. Spoon half of sauce over hens and roast uncovered for an additional 25–30 minutes or until hens reach an internal temperature of 165°. Keep remaining sauce warm until service; add ¼ cup water, if needed, to keep sauce from sticking to pan. Remove hens from baking dish and place on serving platter. Spoon remaining sauce over hens and serve.

Turkey Piccata

Our Lemon Caper Orzo (p. 162) is an excellent side dish with this favorite entrée.

1 lb. boneless fresh turkey breast slices
¼ c. flour
1 T. olive oil
½ c. dry white wine
¼ c. lemon juice
2 T. capers

Lightly coat turkey slices with flour. Heat oil in a medium-size non-stick skillet. Cook turkey 1 ½–2 minutes on each side or until lightly browned. Remove to platter and keep warm. Add the wine and lemon juice to the skillet and bring to a boil, scraping up any brown bits. Add capers. Pour the sauce over the turkey and serve immediately.

Skinless turkey has about one-third less fat than skinless chicken. No wonder it's a part of healthy eating.

Yield:
4 servings

Serving Size:
4 ounces

Preparation Time:
15 minutes

Cooking Time:
6–10 minutes

Nutrition Analysis Per Serving:

Calories 202

Protein 27g

Carbohydrate 8g

Fat 5g

(Saturated 1g)

Cholesterol 56mg

Fiber <1g

Sodium 190mg

Turkey with Pineapple-Cranberry Sauce

There's no doubt about it! Our Sweet Potatoes with Tart Cherries (p. 124) is a must with this meal. Of course, our Praline Sweet Potatoes (p. 123) go well, too.

Yield:
6 servings

Serving Size:
6 ounces turkey and
⅙ of relish

Preparation Time:
20 minutes

Cooking Time:
At least 3 hours

Nutrition Analysis Per Serving:

Calories 452

Protein 60g

Carbohydrate 48g

Fat 2g

(Saturated <1g)

Cholesterol 164mg

Fiber 3g

Sodium 257mg

Pineapple-Cranberry Sauce:
12 oz. fresh or frozen cranberries
1 can (8 oz.) crushed pineapple
in juice, undrained
1 c. sugar, divided
¼ c. orange juice
2 tsp. vanilla extract
1 tsp. grated orange zest

Turkey:
1 (3 lb.) boneless turkey breast
1 tsp. seasoned salt
1 tsp. white pepper

For the sauce, process cranberries, undrained pineapple, ¾ cup of sugar, and orange juice in a food processor container, until coarsely chopped. Pour into non-reactive saucepan. Bring to a boil over medium heat, stirring occasionally; reduce heat. Simmer until thickened, stirring occasionally. Stir in the remaining ¼ cup sugar. Remove from heat. Stir in the vanilla and orange zest. Transfer to a glass or plastic bowl. Cool to room temperature. Cover and chill until serving time.

For the turkey, pat the surface of the meat with the seasoned salt and white pepper. Place the turkey in a baking dish and cover with foil. Insert a meat thermometer through the foil into the thickest portion of the turkey. Bake at 250° for 1 hour per pound or until the thermometer registers 165°. Slice and serve with the chilled relish.

Turkey Wraps with Ginger Slaw

Ginger Slaw:
3 T. rice vinegar
1 T. vegetable oil
1 T. sugar
2 tsp. teriyaki sauce
2 tsp. minced jalapeño pepper
1 tsp. freshly grated ginger root
1 pkg. (16 oz.) coleslaw mix

Turkey Wraps:
1 lb. turkey breast tenderloins
¼ c. teriyaki sauce
1 T. minced garlic
1 tsp. vegetable oil
2 c. cooked rice
4 (10-inch) flour tortillas, warmed
1 c. chopped fresh cilantro

Yield:
4 servings

Serving Size:
1 wrap

Preparation Time:
25 minutes

Cooking Time:
10 minutes

For the slaw, whisk the rice vinegar, oil, sugar, teriyaki sauce, jalapeño, and ginger root in a bowl. Add the coleslaw mix and toss to coat. For wraps, combine the turkey, teriyaki sauce, and garlic in a bowl and mix well. Marinate in the refrigerator for 10 minutes; drain. Pat the turkey with paper towels. Heat the oil in a non-stick skillet. Add the turkey. Cook for 5–7 minutes or until cooked through and brown on both sides, stirring frequently. Spoon ¼ of the rice down the center of each tortilla. Spoon ¼ of the slaw on one side of the rice. Arrange the turkey and cilantro next to the slaw. Fold in the sides of the tortillas and roll to enclose the filling. Cut each wrap into halves before serving.

Nutrition Analysis Per Serving:

Calories 460

Protein 35g

Carbohydrate 58g

Fat 10g

(Saturated 2g)

Cholesterol 56mg

Fiber 3g

Sodium 1160mg

Sweet & Sour Turkey Meatballs

Your guests will love the surprise in each meatball.

Yield:
4 servings

Serving Size:
5 meatballs

Preparation Time:
30–35 minutes

Cooking Time:
30 minutes

1 lb. lean ground turkey
1 egg
⅓ c. finely chopped onion
Salt and black pepper, to taste
5 whole water chestnuts, quartered

Sauce:
¾ c. bottled chili sauce
¼ c. + 2 T. grape jelly

Mix turkey, egg, onion, and seasonings together. Roll mixture into small balls with one-quarter of a water chestnut in the center. Brown in a non-stick skillet. In a large saucepan, mix chili sauce and grape jelly; heat. Add meatballs and simmer for 30 minutes. Serve warm over noodles or rice.

Nutrition Analysis Per Serving:

Calories 258

Protein 30g

Carbohydrate 30g

Fat 3g

(Saturated <1g)

Cholesterol 98mg

Fiber <1g

Sodium 454mg

Water chestnuts are not nuts but tubers (root vegetables). Unlike nuts, they are low in fat and calories.

Leadville Turkey Lasagna

A yummy diversion from traditional lasagna—and easier to make.

1 lb. ground turkey
1 c. chopped onion
2 cloves garlic, minced
1 can (16 oz.) diced tomatoes, undrained
2 cans (8 oz. each) tomato sauce
2 tsp. dried basil leaves
1 tsp. dried oregano leaves
1 tsp. fennel seed
1 egg
2 c. 1% cottage cheese
½ c. grated Parmesan cheese, divided
1 T. dried parsley flakes
½ tsp. black pepper
8 oz. lasagna noodles, uncooked
8 oz. shredded part-skim mozzarella cheese

Preheat oven to 375°. In a large non-stick skillet, brown turkey, onion, and garlic; drain fat. Stir in the next 5 ingredients. Cover and let simmer for 15 minutes, stirring often. Meanwhile, beat egg and combine with cottage cheese, ¼ cup of the Parmesan cheese, parsley, and pepper.

In the bottom of a 13 x 9 x 2-inch baking dish spread ⅓ of the turkey mixture. Rinse noodles with hot water and layer half over meat sauce. Spread half cottage cheese filling over pasta; sprinkle half the mozzarella cheese. Repeat layers ending with remaining turkey mixture. Sprinkle remaining ¼ c. Parmesan cheese on top. Bake for 30–35 minutes until heated through.

Yield:
9 servings

Serving Size:
4 x 3-inch piece

Preparation Time:
30 minutes

Cooking Time:
30–35 minutes

Nutrition Analysis Per Serving:

Calories 318

Protein 33g

Carbohydrate 29g

Fat 8g

(*Saturated 5g*)

Cholesterol 63mg

Fiber 3g

Sodium 740mg

Turkey Enchilada Casserole

Yield:
8 servings

Servings Size:
4 ½ x 3 ¼-inch piece

Preparation Time:
25 minutes

Cooking Time:
25 minutes

1 lb. ground turkey
1 medium onion, chopped
2 cans (8 oz. each) tomato sauce
1 can (12 oz.) mexicorn, drained
1 can (10 oz.) mild enchilada sauce
½ tsp. hot chili powder
¼ tsp. dried oregano leaves
12 corn tortillas
1 ½ c. shredded part-skim mozzarella cheese
1 c. lettuce, shredded
½ c. tomatoes, chopped

Preheat oven to 350°. Cook turkey and onion in a large non-stick skillet until browned; drain fat. Add tomato sauce, mexicorn, enchilada sauce, and seasonings, and mix well. Bring to a boil; reduce heat and simmer for 5 minutes.

Place 6 tortillas in the bottom of a 13 x 9 x 2-inch baking dish. Pour half of the turkey mixture over tortillas; sprinkle with half of the mozzarella cheese. Repeat layers of tortillas and meat. Bake for 20 minutes. Sprinkle with remaining mozzarella cheese and bake an additional 5 minutes. Garnish with lettuce and tomato. (If prepared ahead of time, refrigerate covered. Allow 40 minutes heating time; sprinkle with mozzarella cheese during last 5 minutes in the oven.)

Nutrition Analysis Per Serving:

Calories 305

Protein 23g

Carbohydrate 37g

Fat 7g

(*Saturated 3g*)

Cholesterol 34mg

Fiber 4g

Sodium 807mg

Meats

Beef Tenderloin

So tender it will melt in your mouth.

Yield:
4 servings

Serving Size:
6 ounces

Preparation Time:
5 minutes

Marinating Time:
2 hours

Cooking Time:
10–15 minutes

¼ c. red wine
¼ c. low-sodium soy sauce
¼ tsp. black pepper
¼ tsp. dried whole thyme
⅛ tsp. hot sauce
⅛ tsp. garlic powder
4 (6 oz. each) beef tenderloin steaks

Combine first 6 ingredients; mix well.
Place steaks in a shallow dish; pour wine
mixture over top. Cover and refrigerate
2 hours, turning occasionally. Remove
steaks from marinade and grill over
medium-hot coals to desired doneness.

**Nutrition Analysis
Per Serving:**

Calories 202

Protein 34g

Carbohydrate 1g

Fat 6g

(Saturated 2g)

Cholesterol 90mg

Fiber <1g

Sodium 477mg

*Beef is leaner than ever and easily fits into healthy
eating. The leanest cuts of beef are: eye of round,
top round steak, top sirloin steak, round tip
roast, shoulder pot roast, and shoulder steak.*

Glazed London Broil

This light marinade is lower in sodium than most store-bought versions.

2 lbs. flank steak
1 tsp. unseasoned meat tenderizer
2 T. dry sherry
2 T. low-sodium soy sauce
1 ½ T. honey
¼ tsp. ground ginger

Pierce surface of steak at 1-inch intervals with fork. Combine remaining ingredients and pour over steak. Marinate in a covered container for at least 6 hours in the refrigerator, turning several times. Broil 6 inches from heat for 3 minutes on each side. Cut beef diagonally across the grain; serve warm.

Yield:
6 servings

Serving Size:
5 ounces

Preparation Time:
10 minutes

Marinating Time:
6 hours

Cooking Time:
6–8 minutes

Nutrition Analysis Per Serving:

Calories 284

Protein 33g

Carbohydrate 5g

Fat 13g

(Saturated 6g)

Cholesterol 64mg

Fiber 0g

Sodium 222mg

When selecting meat—think cheap! Cuts of meat are priced by the amount of marbling (fat in the meat fibers) they contain. USDA Select cuts are leaner than Prime or Choice cuts, and cost less.

Steak & Pepper Stir-Fry

Yield:
4 servings

Serving Size:
1 ⅔ cups

Preparation Time:
20 minutes

Cooking Time:
10 minutes

1 lb. beef tip round steak
1 T. cornstarch
¼ tsp. ground ginger
¼ c. low-sodium soy sauce
1 T. peanut oil
3 medium green bell peppers,
cut into 1-inch squares
1 small onion, chopped
1 clove garlic, minced
½ c. water
2 medium tomatoes, cut into wedges
4 c. cooked rice

Slice beef diagonally across the grain into very thin slices. (Meat will slice easier if frozen for 1 hour.) In a small bowl, combine cornstarch and ginger; add soy sauce and stir. Pour soy sauce mixture over beef and stir. Heat oil in wok over medium-high heat. Add beef to wok and stir-fry until brown; remove from pan. Reduce heat and add peppers, onion, garlic, and water to wok; cook 4–5 minutes. Stir in meat and tomatoes; heat throughly. Serve with rice.

Nutrition Analysis Per Serving:

Calories 434

Protein 31g

Carbohydrate 56g

Fat 9g

(Saturated 2g)

Cholesterol 68mg

Fiber 3g

Sodium 470mg

Trimming the fat from a 3-ounce piece of sirloin steak before broiling lowers the amount of fat from 15 grams to 6 grams, and calories from 240 to 150.

Grilled Fajitas

Simply stated, "These are the best fajitas you'll ever taste."

1 c. lowfat Italian dressing
1 can (4 oz.) diced green chiles
1 ½ lb. flank steak
8 flour tortillas, warmed
1 c. shredded lettuce
½ c. diced tomato
⅓ c. shredded reduced-fat
sharp Cheddar cheese
Hot sauce

Combine dressing and green chiles. Pour mixture over flank steak and marinate in a covered glass or ceramic container for at least 6 hours in the refrigerator, turning occasionally. Discard marinade. Grill flank steak 3–4 minutes per side, or until done. Slice steak diagonally across the grain into thin strips. Assemble fajitas by placing a few pieces of meat on a warmed flour tortilla; top with lettuce, tomato, and cheese. Sprinkle with hot sauce (if desired) and roll up.

Variation: Substitute 4 boneless, skinless chicken breasts for flank steak to make chicken fajitas.

Yield:
8 servings

Serving Size:
1 fajita

Preparation Time:
15–20 minutes

Marinating Time:
6 hours

Cooking Time:
10 minutes

Nutrition Analysis Per Serving:

Calories 286

Protein 23g

Carbohydrate 22g

Fat 11g

(Saturated 4g)

Cholesterol 38mg

Fiber 1g

Sodium 381mg

Mexican Beef Stir-Fry

Quick and easy stir-frying techniques are used for this south-of-the-border meal.

Yield:
4 servings

Serving Size:
1 ½ cups

Preparation Time:
20 minutes

Cooking Time:
8–10 minutes

1 lb. lean beef top round steak
1 ½ T. oil
1 tsp. cumin
1 tsp. dried whole oregano leaves
1 clove garlic, minced
1 green bell pepper, cut into thin strips
1 medium onion, cut into thin wedges
1–2 jalapeño peppers, seeded
and cut into slivers
1 tomato, chopped
3 c. sliced romaine lettuce (¼-inch ribbons)
¼ c. shredded, reduced-fat
sharp Cheddar cheese
4 flour tortillas, warmed

**Nutrition Analysis
Per Serving:**

Calories 347

Protein 31g

Carbohydrate 30g

Fat 14g

(*Saturated 4g*)

Cholesterol 55mg

Fiber 3g

Sodium 334mg

Cut beef into thin strips. Combine oil, cumin, oregano, and garlic. Heat half the seasoned oil mixture in a large wok over medium-high heat until hot. Stir-fry beef strips (half at a time) until done; remove from wok and set aside. In remaining oil mixture, stir-fry green pepper, onion, and jalapeños for 1–2 minutes. Add tomato and continue to stir-fry 1 more minute. Return meat to wok with vegetables and heat thoroughly. Spoon beef mixture over lettuce, sprinkle with cheese, and serve with warm tortillas.

The wok is the favored cooking utensil for stir-frying because its sloped sides allow an even distribution of heat and quick cooking. However, a large skillet or an electric skillet also works well.

Pronto Taco Bake

1 lb. lean ground beef
1 pkg. (1 ⅛ oz.) taco seasoning
½ c. water
1 can (12 oz.) whole kernel corn, drained
½ c. chopped green bell pepper
1 can (8 oz.) tomato sauce
Cooking spray
1 pkg. (8 ½ oz.) corn muffin mix
½ c. chopped green onions, divided
⅓ c. shredded part-skim mozzarella cheese

Preheat oven to 400°. In skillet, brown meat; drain. Stir in taco seasoning, water, corn, green pepper, and tomato sauce. Pour into a 12 x 7 ½ x 2-inch baking dish lightly coated with cooking spray. In a separate bowl, prepare corn muffin mix according to package directions; add ¼ cup green onions. Spoon muffin mixture around outer edge of casserole. Bake uncovered for 20 minutes. Top cornbread with cheese and remaining onions; bake 2–3 minutes longer.

Hint: You can lower the sodium content of this dish by deleting the taco seasoning and using chili powder and garlic powder.

Yield:
6 servings

Serving Size:
4 x 3 ¾-inch piece

Preparation Time:
15 minutes

Cooking Time:
25 minutes

Nutrition Analysis Per Serving:

Calories 386

Protein 21g

Carbohydrate 44g

Fat 13g

(Saturated 5g)

Cholesterol 61mg

Fiber 3g

Sodium 1074mg

Durango Short Ribs with Noodles

A one-pot meal that requires only a tossed salad to make a feast.

Yield:
8 servings

Serving Size:
1 ½ cups

Preparation Time:
10 minutes

Cooking Time:
2 hours, 20 minutes

3 lbs. lean boneless beef short ribs
2 medium onions, sliced
1 can (15 oz.) tomato sauce
1 c. water
¼ c. packed brown sugar
¼ c. vinegar
1 tsp. dry mustard
1 tsp. Worcestershire sauce
½ tsp. salt
2 c. linguine noodles, uncooked
1 c. water

In a large non-stick skillet, brown meat; drain fat. Add onions to meat and continue to cook 1 more minute. Blend together tomato sauce, water, brown sugar, vinegar, dry mustard, Worcestershire sauce, and salt. Pour mixture over meat. Cover and simmer for 2 hours or until meat is tender. Skim off fat; sir in uncooked noodles and second cup of water. Cover and cook, stirring occasionally, for 15–20 minutes more, or until noodles are tender.

Nutrition Analysis Per Serving:

Calories 714

Protein 60g

Carbohydrate 45g

Fat 32g

(Saturated 13g)

Cholesterol 158mg

Fiber 3g

Sodium 502mg

When sautéing or frying, make sure your cooking oil is hot before adding ingredients. Foods soak up cool oil faster than hot oil. One extra tablespoon of oil absorbed by foods adds 100 calories to the total.

Smoky Beef Brisket

2 T. liquid smoke
2 tsp. celery seed
1 tsp. garlic powder
1 tsp. onion powder
1 tsp. Worcestershire sauce
3 lb. lean brisket
½ tsp. salt
½ tsp. freshly ground black pepper
1 c. your favorite barbecue sauce

Mix liquid smoke, celery seed, garlic powder,
onion powder, and Worcestershire sauce.
Rub both sides of brisket with mixture;
place in a covered baking dish and marinate
overnight in the refrigerator. To cook, preheat
the oven to 300°. Sprinkle brisket with
salt and pepper; cover with foil and bake
for 4 hours. Add barbecue sauce and bake
uncovered for 1 hour, basting occasionally.

Yield:
8 servings

Serving Size:
4 ounces

Preparation Time:
10 minutes

Marinating Time:
6–10 hours

Cooking Time:
5 hours

**Nutrition Analysis
Per Serving:**

Calories 239

Protein 37g

Carbohydrate 5g

Fat 7g

(Saturated 2g)

Cholesterol 65mg

Fiber 1g

Sodium 537mg

San Luis Barbecued Beef with Beans

The nutritional benefits of beans are endless. Introduce your family to more beans with this popular casserole.

Yield:
8 servings

Serving Size:
1 ¼ cups

Preparation Time:
20 minutes

Cooking Time:
1 hour

¾ lb. lean ground beef
¾ c. chopped onion
½ c. chopped celery
2 cans (15 oz. each) baked beans
1 can (15 oz.) kidney beans, drained and rinsed
1 can (15 oz.) butter or lima beans, drained and rinsed
½ c. ketchup
⅓ c. packed brown sugar
2 T. red wine vinegar
1 tsp. dry mustard

Preheat oven to 350°. In a large non-tick skillet, brown beef, adding onion and celery during the last 4 minutes of the browning process. Stir frequently. Drain fat. Add beans to meat mixture. In a separate bowl, mix together ketchup, sugar, vinegar, and mustard. Fold sauce into meat and beans, being careful not to crush beans. Pour mixture into a 2-quart casserole dish and bake for 1 hour.

Nutrition Analysis Per Serving:

Calories 335

Protein 20g

Carbohydrate 55g

Fat 5g

(Saturated 2g)

Cholesterol 28mg

Fiber 13g

Sodium 382mg

Increase the fiber in your diet gradually. Too much fiber too fast may result in abdominal discomfort.

Rancher's Meat Loaf

Go ahead, try something new for dinner—like buffalo!

1 lb. lean ground buffalo
⅔ c. regular oats, uncooked
⅓ c. your favorite barbecue sauce
1 egg
¼ c. chopped onion
¼ c. chopped green pepper
1 T. dried parsley flakes
2 tsp. Worcestershire sauce
Cooking spray

Preheat oven to 350°. Combine all ingredients and place in a 9 x 5 x 3-inch pan coated with cooking spray. Bake for 45–50 minutes or until done.

Buffalo is naturally flavorful and lean. Ground buffalo can be used in many recipes in place of ground beef.

Yield:
4 servings

Serving Size:
4 ounces

Preparation Time:
10–15 minutes

Cooking Time:
45–50 minutes

Nutrition Analysis Per Serving:

Calories 232

Protein 28g

Carbohydrate 14g

Fat 7g

(Saturated 2g)

Cholesterol 108mg

Fiber 2g

Sodium 267mg

Lemon Ginger-Glazed Lamb Chops

Yield:
4 servings

Serving Size:
2 lamb chops

Preparation Time:
5 minutes

Cooking Time:
10–15 minutes

½ c. pineapple juice
½ c. packed brown sugar
2 tsp. minced fresh ginger root,
or 1 tsp. ground ginger
2 tsp. grated lemon peel
Salt and black pepper, to taste
8 lamb chops, 1-inch thick

In a saucepan, combine pineapple juice, brown sugar, ginger, lemon peel, salt, and pepper. Cook over medium heat until sugar dissolves. Brush both sides of lamb chops with glaze and arrange chops on broiler rack. Broil 6 inches from heat for 5–7 minutes, or to desired doneness. Brush frequently with glaze.

Nutrition Analysis Per Serving:

Calories 308

Protein 27g

Carbohydrate 31g

Fat 8g

(Saturated 3g)

Cholesterol 86mg

Fiber <1g

Sodium 100mg

When grating or zesting lemon, lime, or orange peel, grate extra and store it in the freezer.

Royal Gorge Roast Rack of Lamb

Simple, yet elegant. Save this entrée for someone you really want to impress.

**1 rack of lamb (about 2 lbs.,
12 ribs), well trimmed
1 ½ tsp. stone-ground mustard
⅓ c. dry breadcrumbs
2 T. chopped fresh parsley
½ tsp. dried rosemary leaves
¼ tsp. black pepper**

Preheat oven to 375°. On roasting rack in shallow baking pan, place lamb roast, meaty side up. Spread mustard over meat. Combine breadcrumbs, parsley, rosemary, and pepper. Pat mixture over mustard. Roast until desired doneness: an internal temperature of 145° for rare, 160° for medium, or 170° for well-done. Let roast stand for 10 minutes before carving.

Yield:
6 servings

Serving Size:
2 ribs

Preparation Time:
5–10 minutes

Cooking Time:
1 hour, 10 minutes

**Nutrition Analysis
Per Serving:**

Calories 280

Protein 31g

Carbohydrate 5g

Fat 14g

(Saturated 5g)

Cholesterol 100mg

Fiber <1g

Sodium 170mg

Spicy Grilled Pork Chops

A barbecue sensation!

Yield:
4 servings

Serving Size:
4 ounces

Preparation Time:
5 minutes

Marinating Time:
1 hour

Cooking Time:
8–10 minutes

Nutrition Analysis Per Serving:

Calories 189

Protein 27g

Carbohydrate 6g

Fat 6g

(Saturated 2g)

Cholesterol 83mg

Fiber <1g

Sodium 203mg

¼ c. thick and chunky hot salsa
2 T. water
2 T. orange marmalade
¼ tsp. seasoned salt
4 boneless, center-cut pork loin chops, ½-inch thick, trimmed (about 1 lb.)

In a small bowl, combine salsa, water, marmalade, and salt; blend well. Place pork chops in plastic bag or non-metal baking dish. Pour marinade mixture over pork, turning to coat. Seal bag or cover dish; marinate 1 hour, turning pork chops several times. Remove pork chops from marinade. Place chops on grill 4–6 inches from medium-hot coals. Grill about 4 minutes per side.

Pork Chops in Apple Juice

4 boneless, center-cut pork
loin chops (about 1 lb.)
Cooking spray
¼ tsp. dried whole sage
Salt and black pepper, to taste
1 c. apple juice
¼ c. raisins

Preheat oven to 350°. Trim any excess fat
from pork chops; brown in a non-stick
skillet coated with cooking spray. Arrange
in baking dish (single layer if possible).
Sprinkle chops with sage, salt, and pepper;
pour apple juice over chops. Cover and bake
about 1 hour or until meat is tender. Add
raisins during last half hour of baking.

Hint: Pork chops can be simmered in a
covered pan on a stove, if preferred.

*For food safety, the FDA recommends cooking
lean pork to an internal temperature of 155° for
medium doneness. At this temperature, pork will
be tender, juicy, and slightly pink in the middle.*

Yield:
4 servings

Serving Size:
4 ounces

Preparation Time:
10 minutes

Cooking Time:
1 hour

**Nutrition Analysis
Per Serving:**

Calories 204

Protein 16g

Carbohydrate 14g

Fat 9g

(Saturated 3g)

Cholesterol 53mg

Fiber <1g

Sodium 53mg

Sesame Pork with Broccoli

This is a perfect one-dish Sunday supper after a weekend in the mountains.

Yield:
4 servings

Serving Size:
1 ½ cups

Preparation Time:
5 minutes

Cooking Time:
10–15 minutes

1 can (14 ½ oz.) chicken broth
2 T. cornstarch
1 T. low-sodium soy sauce
4 green onions, chopped
1 lb. pork tenderloin, trimmed
1 T. peanut oil
1 clove garlic, minced
1 ½ lb. fresh broccoli florets
2 T. sesame seeds, lightly toasted

In a small bowl, combine the chicken broth, cornstarch, and soy sauce; blend well. Stir in green onions; set aside. Cut pork tenderloin into bite-size pieces. Heat oil in wok. Add pork and garlic; stir-fry for 4–5 minutes or until pork is done. Remove pork; keep warm. Add broccoli and broth mixture to wok. Cover and simmer over low heat for 6 minutes. Add cooked pork; cook just until mixture is hot, stirring frequently. Sprinkle with sesame seeds; serve immediately.

Nutrition Analysis Per Serving:

Calories 276

Protein 31g

Carbohydrate 16g

Fat 10g

(Saturated 2g)

Cholesterol 74mg

Fiber 6g

Sodium 378mg

A serving of broccoli (about 1 cup) contains more vitamin C than an orange—more than enough to meet the Recommended Dietary Allowance.

Carne Adovada

A spicy traditional dish for those who like it hot.

¼ c. hot chili powder
¼ c. mild chili powder
2 cloves garlic, minced
1 T. cumin
1 T. dried oregano leaves
½ tsp. salt
1 ½ c. water
3 lb. lean center-cut pork chops,
trimmed of visible fat

Combine all ingredients except pork. Place pork chops in a 12 x 7 ½ x 2-inch baking dish. Pour chili mixture over chops and bake at 325° for 45 minutes. Uncover and continue to bake 30 more minutes. Let cool and shred pork. Serve with flour tortillas, lettuce, and plain nonfat or lowfat yogurt, if desired.

Recipes containing chili powder may not need much salt since salt is one of the ingredients in most commercial chili powders.

Yield:
8 servings

Serving Size:
5 ounces

Preparation Time:
10 minutes

Cooking Time:
1 ¼ hours

Nutrition Analysis Per Serving:

Calories 272

Protein 39g

Carbohydrate 5g

Fat 11g

(Saturated 3g)

Cholesterol 105mg

Fiber 3.2g

Sodium 340mg

Jalapeño Honey Pork Tenderloin

Yield:
6 servings

Serving Size:
6 ounces

Preparation Time:
5 minutes

Marinating Time:
8 hours

Cooking Time:
30 minutes

Nutrition Analysis Per Serving:

Calories 228

Protein 25g

Carbohydrate 17g

Fat 6g

(*Saturated 2g*)

Cholesterol 67mg

Fiber <1g

Sodium 302mg

⅓ c. honey
3 T. low-sodium soy sauce
1 T. sesame oil
2 jalapeño chiles, seeded and finely chopped
1 T. grated fresh ginger root
¼ tsp. red pepper flakes
2 (12 oz.) pork tenderloins

Combine the honey, soy sauce, sesame oil, chiles, ginger root, and red pepper flakes in a 1-gallon sealable plastic bag. Add the pork and seal tightly. Shake to coat. Marinate in the refrigerator for 8 hours, turning occasionally; drain. Grill the pork over medium-hot coals until a meat thermometer inserted in the thickest portion of the pork registers 145°. Remove the pork to a cutting board and let stand, covered, for 10 minutes. Cut diagonally into ¼-inch slices; serve.

Tip: If you do not have access to a grill, or prefer to cook indoors, place the pork on a rack in a roasting pan. Bake at 425° for 30 minutes or until a meat thermometer registers 145°.

Wear latex gloves to keep the oil off your hands when chopping or working with jalapeño chiles or any type of hot peppers. Your skin, especially around the eyes, is very sensitive to the oil from the hot peppers.

Vegetarian Entrées

Cranberry-Glazed Tempeh

If you like tempeh, you will love this recipe.

Yield:
4 servings

Serving Size:
4 ounces
(2 triangles)

Preparation Time:
15–20 minutes

Cooking Time:
50–55 minutes

2 pkgs. (8 oz. each) wild rice tempeh
1 can (15 oz.) whole cranberry sauce
½ c. water
2 T. maple syrup
1 T. soy sauce
1 T. dry sherry
1 T. grated fresh ginger root,
or 1 tsp. ground ginger
¼ tsp. allspice
¼ tsp. cinnamon
¼ tsp. salt
⅛ tsp. nutmeg
Cayenne pepper, to taste

Preheat oven to 350°. Cut each block of tempeh into 4 triangles. Steam the tempeh in a steamer basket for 10 minutes. Arrange in a single layer in a baking dish. Combine the cranberry sauce, water, maple syrup, soy sauce, sherry, ginger root, allspice, cinnamon, salt, nutmeg, and cayenne pepper in a blender or food processor. Process until smooth. Strain the sauce through fine mesh strainer to remove the seeds, for a smoother sauce. Pour over the tempeh. Bake for 40–45 minutes.

Tempeh is a flat cake made from fermented soybeans. Unlike tofu, which absorbs the flavors of the foods with which it is cooked, tempeh has a smoky flavor and a chewy texture. Here are some suggestions: Grill tempeh after marinating it in a sauce; chop tempeh and mix it in casseroles, chili, or soups; or grill tempeh and top it with burger fixings.

Nutrition Analysis Per Serving:

Calories 409

Protein 22g

Carbohydrate 66g

Fat 9g

(Saturated 1g)

Cholesterol 0mg

Fiber 8g

Sodium 505mg

Grilled Tofu Steaks

1 lb. firm tofu, cut lengthwise into 4 steaks
¼ c. low-sodium soy sauce
¼ c. red wine vinegar
1 tsp. olive oil
1 tsp. sesame oil
½ tsp. dried oregano leaves
¼ tsp. garlic powder
⅛ tsp. ground ginger
Cayenne pepper, to taste

Place the tofu on a plate lined with paper towels. Cover the tofu with additional paper towels. Top with a plate. Weight with several canned goods or a cast-iron skillet to press out excess moisture. Let stand for 20 minutes. Combine the soy sauce, wine vinegar, olive oil, sesame oil, oregano, garlic powder, ginger, and pepper in a shallow dish and mix well. Add the tofu steaks, turning to coat. Marinate, covered, in the refrigerator for 6 hours or longer, turning once; drain. Grill over medium-hot coals for 6 minutes per side or until brown. May broil if desired. Serve with rice or another whole grain for a filling meal.

Pressing the moisture out of the tofu allows it to become firm and absorb flavors in the sauce.

Yield:
4 servings

Serving Size:
1 steak

Preparation Time:
10 minutes

Marinating Time:
6 hours

Cooking Time:
12 minutes

Nutrition Analysis Per Serving:

Calories 110

Protein 9g

Carbohydrate 5g

Fat 5g

(*Saturated 1g*)

Cholesterol 0mg

Fiber <1g

Sodium 547mg

Vegetable Tofu Curry

Yield:
5 servings

Serving Size:
1 cup

Preparation Time:
25 minutes

Cooking Time:
40 minutes

3 c. water
3 potatoes, peeled and cubed
3 carrots, cut into ¼-inch slices
1 tsp. salt
1 ½ T. canola oil
1 large onion, chopped
1 large apple, sliced
⅓ c. raisins
8 oz. firm tofu, cubed
2 T. flour
2 T. curry powder
1 ½ tsp. cinnamon
2 tsp. low-sodium soy sauce

**Nutrition Analysis
Per Serving:**

Calories 227

Protein 7g

Carbohydrate 39g

Fat 6g

(*Saturated 1g*)

Cholesterol 0mg

Fiber 5g

Sodium 572mg

Bring the water to a boil in a 4-quart saucepan. Add the potatoes, carrots, and salt. Cook for 15 minutes or until the vegetables are tender. Drain, reserving the vegetable broth. Return the vegetables to the saucepan. Cover to keep warm. Heat the canola oil in a large skillet over medium-high heat. Add the onion. Sauté for 5 minutes or until tender; reduce heat. Stir in the apple and raisins.

Cook over low heat for 10 minutes, stirring occasionally. Add the tofu and mix well. Cook for 5 minutes, stirring frequently. Sprinkle the flour, curry powder, and cinnamon over the tofu mixture and mix well. Stir in the reserved vegetable broth and soy sauce. Cook until thickened, stirring constantly. Add to the potatoes and carrots and mix gently. Serve over hot cooked basmati rice, with chutney on the side.

Telluride Tofu & Mushrooms

Mushrooms provide a meaty texture for this meatless dish.

4 c. hot cooked rice
1 lb. firm tofu
½ c. low-sodium soy sauce
1 T. brown sugar
1 T. olive oil
2 c. sliced fresh mushrooms
2 cloves garlic, minced
1 large tomato, chopped
¼ c. chopped green onions

Yield:
4 servings

Serving Size:
1 cup rice and ½ cup stir-fry

Preparation Time:
20–25 minutes

Cooking Time:
10 minutes

Prepare rice according to package directions, and set aside. Place the tofu block on a plate lined with paper towels. Cover the tofu with additional paper towels. Top with a plate. Weight with several canned goods or a cast-iron skillet to press out excess moisture. Let stand for 20 minutes. Combine the soy sauce and brown sugar in a small bowl and mix well. Heat the olive oil in a large non-stick skillet. Add the mushrooms and garlic. Sauté over medium heat until the mushrooms are tender. Cut the tofu into ½-inch cubes. Stir into the mushroom mixture. Add the soy sauce mixture, tomato, and green onions and mix well. Cook for 5 minutes, stirring frequently. Spoon over the rice on a serving platter.

Firm and extra-firm tofu hold their texture and shape and are best in salads, stir-fry, and in recipes that call for meat or chicken. Soft tofu is moist and can be used for dressings and dips, or as a substitute for soft cheeses, such as ricotta.

Nutrition Analysis Per Serving:

Calories 370

Protein 16g

Carbohydrate 60g

Fat 7g

(*Saturated 1g*)

Cholesterol 0mg

Fiber 2g

Sodium 1061mg

Mesa Verde Black Beans with Rice

Yield:
6 servings

Serving Size:
1 cup

Preparation Time:
15–20 minutes

Cooking Time:
30 minutes

4 ½ c. cooked long-grain rice
Cooking spray
1 c. chopped onion
1 c. chopped green bell pepper
4 cloves garlic, minced
2 cans (15 oz. each) black beans, drained
2 c. water
¼ tsp. crushed red pepper flakes
¼ tsp. salt
1 can (6 oz.) tomato paste
1 T. vinegar
½ c. chopped tomatoes
¼ c. chopped green onions
¼ c. plain nonfat or lowfat yogurt

**Nutrition Analysis
Per Serving:**

Calories 332

Protein 12g

Carbohydrate 75g

Fat <1g

(Saturated <1g)

Cholesterol <1mg

Fiber 9g

Sodium 414mg

Prepare long-grain rice according to package directions; set aside. Coat a large pot with cooking spray. Place over medium heat; add onion, green pepper, and garlic; sauté until tender, stirring often. Add black beans, water, crushed red pepper flakes, and salt. Bring to a boil; cover, reduce heat, and simmer 15 minutes, stirring occasionally. Add tomato paste and vinegar; uncover and cook 15 minutes longer or until thickened. Serve over ¾ cup rice and top evenly with chopped tomatoes, green onions, and yogurt.

The acid in tomatoes and vinegar toughens beans—that's why these ingredients usually are added last.

Boulder Burritos

These make a great grab-and-go meal, and are an adventurous way to add more greens to your diet.

1 c. water
½ c. bulgur
1 large onion, chopped
4 cloves garlic, minced
3 T. olive oil
6 c. chopped kale
1 can (15 oz.) pinto beans, drained and rinsed
2 T. lemon juice
2 tsp. cumin
8 (10-inch) flour tortillas
1 c. your favorite salsa
1 c. shredded, reduced-fat Cheddar cheese

Yield:
8 servings

Serving Size:
1 burrito

Preparation Time:
20–25 minutes

Cooking Time:
40 minutes

Combine water and bulgur in a saucepan and mix well. Simmer for 20 minutes or until tender. In a skillet, sauté the onion and garlic in olive oil until tender. Stir in the kale and sauté until wilted. Add bulgur, beans, lemon juice, and cumin; mix well. Cook until heated through, stirring occasionally. Remove from heat. Spoon ⅛ of the bean mixture onto each tortilla. Top each with 2 tablespoons of the salsa and 2 tablespoons of the cheese. Roll to enclose the filling. Arrange seam side down in a 9 x 13 x 2-inch baking dish. Bake, covered, at 350° for 15 minutes or until heated through—or microwave on medium for 3 to 4 minutes.

To please vegetarians and non-vegetarians alike, center meals around entrées that are not typically thought of as vegetarian, such as soups and sandwiches, pasta with marinara sauce, macaroni and cheese, vegetable "fried" rice, or bean burritos.

Nutrition Analysis Per Serving:

Calories 423

Protein 16g

Carbohydrate 64g

Fat 12g

(Saturated 3g)

Cholesterol 3mg

Fiber 8g

Sodium 751mg

Black Bean Tortilla Casserole

Yield:
6 servings

Serving Size:
4 ½ x 4 ½-inch piece

Preparation Time:
25 minutes

Cooking Time:
50 minutes

**Nutrition Analysis
Per Serving:**

Calories 389

Protein 22g

Carbohydrate 57g

Fat 9g

(Saturated 4g)

Cholesterol 20mg

Fiber 14g

Sodium 942mg

Cooking spray
1 c. chopped onion
2 c. chopped red and green bell peppers
2 cloves garlic, minced
2 cans (15 oz.) black beans, drained and rinsed
1 can (14 oz.) no-salt-added diced
tomatoes, undrained
1 c. your favorite picante sauce
1 T. cumin
12 (6-inch) corn tortillas
1 ½ c. shredded, reduced-fat
Monterey Jack cheese
2 c. shredded lettuce
½ c. chopped tomato
⅓ c. light sour cream

Spray a large, non-stick skillet with cooking spray. Sauté onion; add bell peppers and garlic and mix well. Sauté for 3 minutes or until peppers are tender. Stir in beans, undrained tomatoes, picante sauce, and cumin. Cook for 5 minutes, stirring occasionally. Remove from heat.

Lightly coat a 9 x 13 x 2-inch baking pan with cooking spray. Spread 1 cup bean mixture in pan. Arrange 6 tortillas over bean mixture. Spread with ¾ cup cheese. Spoon 2 ½ cups bean mixture over cheese. Top with 6 more tortillas and add remaining bean mixture. Bake, covered, at 350° for 30 minutes; sprinkle with remaining ¾ cup cheese. Bake until cheese melts. Let stand for 5 minutes before serving then cut into 6 portions. Top with lettuce, tomato, and sour cream.

Spinach Enchilada Casserole

1 medium onion, chopped
Cooking spray
1 pkg. (10 oz.) frozen chopped spinach, thawed
2 cans (8 oz. each) tomato sauce
1 can (12 oz.) mexicorn, drained
1 can (10 oz.) mild enchilada sauce
1 tsp. chili powder
¼ tsp. dried oregano leaves
12 corn tortillas
6 oz. shredded part-skim mozzarella cheese
1 c. shredded lettuce
½ c. chopped fresh tomatoes

Yield:
8 servings

Serving Size:
4 ½ x 3 ¼-inch piece

Preparation Time:
25 minutes

Cooking Time:
25 minutes

Preheat oven to 350°. Sauté onion in a large non-stick skillet coated with cooking spray. Drain spinach and pat out excess moisture between paper towels. In a saucepan, combine onion, spinach, tomato sauce, mexicorn, enchilada sauce, and seasonings; mix well. Bring to a boil; reduce heat and simmer for 5 minutes. Place 6 tortillas in the bottom of a 9 x 13 x 2-inch baking dish.

Pour half of spinach mixture over tortillas; sprinkle with one-half of mozzarella cheese. Repeat the layers, using tortillas and spinach mixture. Bake for 20 minutes. Sprinkle with remaining mozzarella cheese and bake an additional 5 minutes. Garnish with lettuce and tomato. (If prepared ahead of time, refrigerate covered. Allow 40 minutes heating time; sprinkle with mozzarella cheese during last 5 minutes of baking.)

Nutrition Analysis Per Serving:

Calories 184

Protein 10g

Carbohydrate 26g

Fat 5g

(Saturated 2g)

Cholesterol 14mg

Fiber 3g

Sodium 805mg

Spinach Quesadillas

Yield:
4 servings

Serving Size:
1 quesadilla

Preparation Time:
15–20 minutes

Cooking Time:
25 minutes

1 pkg. (10 oz.) frozen chopped spinach
2 T. minced onion
2 T. minced garlic
2 T. minced mushrooms
2 T. minced fresh jalapeño chiles
2 T. minced fresh cilantro
8 (6-inch) corn tortillas
Cooking spray
4 oz. fat-free or regular refried beans
¼ c. shredded mozzarella cheese
Salsa Fresca, (p. 10)

Combine the spinach with a small amount of water in a microwave-safe dish. Microwave, covered, on high for 5 minutes or until the spinach is thawed; drain. Squeeze the excess moisture from the spinach by placing it between paper towels and gently patting it down. Combine the spinach, onion, garlic, mushrooms, chiles, and cilantro in a bowl and mix well.

Arrange 4 of the tortillas in a single layer on a baking sheet coated with cooking spray. Spread the tortillas with the refried beans. Spread with the spinach mixture and sprinkle with cheese. Top with the remaining tortillas. Bake at 375° for 15–20 minutes or until light brown. Serve with salsa.

Variation: Try making these with *Santa Fe Beans,* (p. 147).

Nutrition Analysis Per Serving:

Calories 200

Protein 9g

Carbohydrate 37g

Fat 3g

(Saturated 1g)

Cholesterol 6mg

Fiber 7g

Sodium 274mg

Twice-Baked Potato Dinner

Bake extra potatoes to have them ready for this scrumptious entrée.

2 large potatoes, baked
6 T. skim milk
½ c. 1% cottage cheese
¼ c. chopped green pepper
¼ c. chopped carrots
¼ c. chopped green onions
2 T. sunflower seeds
½ c. shredded reduced-fat
sharp Cheddar cheese
¼ tsp. garlic salt
¼ tsp. black pepper
6 cherry tomatoes, halved

Yield:
4 servings

Serving Size:
½ potato

Preparation Time:
20 minutes

Cooking Time:
10–12 minutes

Preheat oven to 450°. Halve the baked potatoes and scoop out pulp, leaving ¼ inch remaining in shells. Mash potato pulp in a bowl. Add milk, cottage cheese, green pepper, carrot, onion, sunflower seeds, half the Cheddar cheese, salt, and pepper. Gently mix to blend thoroughly. Mound into potato shells, dividing equally. Arrange 3 cherry tomato halves on each potato half, pushing them in slightly. Sprinkle with remaining Cheddar cheese. Bake for 10–12 minutes or until cheese is melted and potatoes are heated thoroughly.

Hint: Potatoes may be prepared in advance up to the point of heating. Wrap them securely and refrigerate up to 2 days. Reheat in a conventional oven, as directed above, or heat them in a microwave, according to manufacturer's directions.

Nutrition Analysis Per Serving:

Calories 202

Protein 11g

Carbohydrate 27g

Fat 6g

(Saturated 2g)

Cholesterol 9mg

Fiber 3g

Sodium 304mg

Sesame Chick-Pea Dinner Wraps

Yield:
6 servings

Serving Size:
1 wrap

Preparation Time:
15 minutes

2 T. sesame seeds
1 can (15 oz.) chick-peas, drained and rinsed
6 c. slivered romaine lettuce
1 red bell pepper, finely chopped
4 oz. reduced-fat feta cheese, crumbled
3 T. lemon juice
1 T. olive oil
1 T. chopped fresh basil, or 1 tsp. dried basil
1 tsp. minced garlic
½ tsp. freshly ground black pepper
6 (10-inch) flour tortillas, heated

Toast the sesame seeds in an ungreased skillet over medium heat until golden brown and fragrant, stirring frequently. Process the chick-peas in a blender or food processor until coarsely chopped. Toss romaine and red pepper in a salad bowl. Add the feta cheese and chick peas and mix well. Sprinkle with sesame seeds. Whisk the lemon juice, olive oil, basil, garlic, and pepper in a bowl. Drizzle over the romaine mixture, tossing to coat. Spoon 1 cup of the romaine mixture in the center of each tortilla. Roll to enclose the filling.

**Nutrition Analysis
Per Serving:**

Calories 423

Protein 14g

Carbohydrate 61g

Fat 14g

(Saturated 5g)

Cholesterol 17mg

Fiber 7g

Sodium 773mg

*Sesame seeds and olive oil are good
sources of monounsaturated fats, which
help lower blood cholesterol levels.*

Vegetable Calzones

1 loaf (1 lb.) frozen bread dough,
white or whole-wheat
2 tsp. olive oil
1 c. sliced fresh mushrooms
¾ c. chopped red bell pepper
½ c. chopped onion
1 pkg. (10 oz.) frozen chopped spinach, thawed
1 c. light ricotta cheese
¼ c. grated Parmesan cheese
1 c. (4 oz.) shredded part-
skim mozzarella cheese
½ tsp. Italian seasoning
Cooking spray
2 c. your favorite spaghetti sauce

Yield:
4 servings

Serving Size:
1 calzone

Preparation Time:
30 minutes

Cooking Time:
15–20 minutes

Let bread dough rise according to package directions. Preheat oven to 400°. Heat olive oil in a nonstick skillet over medium heat; add mushrooms, red pepper, and onion. Sauté until tender; remove from heat. Drain spinach and squeeze out excess moisture. Combine spinach, cheeses, and Italian seasoning; mix well. Add sautéed vegetables and mix well.

Punch bread dough down and divide into 4 equal portions. Shape each portion into an 8-inch circle. Spoon ⅔ cup vegetable and cheese mixture onto ½ of each circle, leaving a ½-inch border. Moisten edges of circle with water. Fold plain half of each circle over filling, crimping edges to seal. Place calzones on baking sheet coated with cooking spray. Bake 15–20 minutes or until golden brown. Serve with ½ c. spaghetti sauce for dipping.

Nutrition Analysis Per Serving:

Calories 631

Protein 33g

Carbohydrate 79g

Fat 22g

(Saturated 6g)

Cholesterol 24mg

Fiber 8g

Sodium 1526mg

Portobello Mushroom Sandwiches

Yield:
4 servings

Serving Size:
1 sandwich

Preparation Time:
10 minutes

Marinating Time:
20–30 minutes

Cooking Time:
10 minutes

**Nutrition Analysis
Per Serving:**

Calories 410

Protein 18g

Carbohydrate 58g

Fat 13g

(Saturated 5g)

Cholesterol 15mg

Fiber 8g

Sodium 856mg

½ c. balsamic vinegar
¼ c. Worcestershire sauce
2 green onions, finely chopped
1 T. olive oil
1 tsp. crushed dried rosemary
4 Portobello mushrooms, stems removed
4 Kaiser rolls, split
2 oz. goat or feta cheese, crumbled
⅓ c. roasted red bell pepper slices
1 c. fresh spinach leaves

Combine the balsamic vinegar, Worcestershire sauce, green onions, olive oil, and rosemary in a sealable plastic bag. Add the mushrooms and seal tightly. Toss to coat. Marinate at room temperature for 20–30 minutes, turning occasionally; drain. Grill the mushrooms over medium-hot coals for 4–6 minutes per side. Place the rolls on the grill rack. Grill for 2–3 minutes. Layer the cheese, mushroom caps, red pepper, and spinach (in the order listed) on the bottom roll halves. Top with the remaining roll halves. Serve with a salad of mixed greens.

Roasting peppers is easily done individually or in quantity. To roast a single pepper, secure the pepper with a long-handled fork or skewer. Turn a stove-top burner to high and rotate the pepper until it is evenly charred. Place the pepper in a paper bag and seal tightly. When cooled, remove the charred skin. To roast several peppers, broil in oven or toaster oven, turning frequently. Or grill the peppers over hot coals until charred and blistered.

Portobello Mushrooms Florentine

4 whole Portobello mushrooms,
stems and black "ribs" removed
½ tsp. olive oil
1 pkg. (10 oz.) frozen chopped
spinach, thawed and drained
¼ c. chopped onion
3 T. dry breadcrumbs
2 tsp. grated Parmesan cheese
1 tsp. garlic powder
1 tsp. dried oregano leaves
1 egg, lightly beaten
¼ c. shredded mozzarella cheese

Arrange the mushrooms with top sides down
on a baking sheet. Heat the olive oil in a large
non-stick skillet over medium heat. Add the
spinach and onion and mix well. Sauté for 10
minutes or until the onion is tender. Stir in the
breadcrumbs, Parmesan cheese, garlic powder,
and oregano. Remove from heat. Stir in the egg.
Spoon equal portions of the spinach mixture
onto each mushroom and pat firmly. Top each
with 1 tablespoon of mozzarella cheese. Bake at
375° for 15–20 minutes or until light brown.

Yield:
4 servings

Serving Size:
1 mushroom cap

Preparation Time:
20 minutes

Cooking Time:
25–30 minutes

**Nutrition Analysis
Per Serving:**

Calories 139

Protein 14g

Carbohydrate 18g

Fat 4g

(Saturated 2g)

Cholesterol 59mg

Fiber 10g

Sodium 183mg

Eggplant Parmesan

Yield:
6 servings

Serving Size:
4 ½ x 4 ⅓-inch piece

Preparation Time:
15–20 minutes

Cooking Time:
30 minutes

Nutrition Analysis Per Serving:

Calories 237

Protein 14g

Carbohydrate 27g

Fat 9g

(*Saturated 4g*)

Cholesterol 20mg

Fiber 2g

Sodium 933mg

1–3 T. flour
1 lb. eggplant
2 egg whites
2 T. skim milk
⅔ c. Italian breadcrumbs
Cooking spray
1 jar (26 oz.) your favorite spaghetti sauce
1 ½ c. (6 oz.) shredded part-skim mozzarella cheese
3 T. grated Parmesan cheese

Preheat oven to 400°. Place flour in a large sealable plastic bag; set aside. Peel and cut eggplant into ½-inch thick slices (approximately 12). Place slices in plastic bag; shake to coat. Combine egg whites and milk. Dip each eggplant slice into egg white mixture and lightly coat them on all sides with Italian breadcrumbs. Place slices on a baking sheet coated with cooking spray. Bake 12–15 minutes or until lightly browned and tender. Reduce oven temperature to 350°.

Lightly coat a 13 x 9 x 2-inch baking dish with cooking spray. Place half the eggplant slices in a single layer on the bottom of the dish. Spoon half the spaghetti sauce over the slices and sprinkle with half the mozzarella cheese. Repeat, adding a second layer with the remaining ingredients. Top with Parmesan cheese and bake uncovered 15 minutes, or until thoroughly heated.

Mouthwatering Manicotti

1 jar (26 oz.) your favorite spaghetti sauce
1 can (16 oz.) diced tomatoes, undrained
1 clove garlic, minced
2 c. 1% cottage cheese
1 c. light ricotta cheese
3 T. Parmesan cheese
2 egg whites
4 T. chopped fresh parsley
8 oz. manicotti shells (14 shells), uncooked
1 c. water

Yield:
7 servings

Serving Size:
2 manicotti

Preparation Time:
20 minutes

Cooking Time:
1 hour

Preheat oven to 450°. Combine spaghetti sauce, tomatoes, and garlic; set aside. Combine cheeses, egg whites, and parsley; stuff uncooked manicotti shells with cheese mixture using a small spatula. Fill bottom of a 12 x 7 x 2-inch casserole dish with 2 cups tomato mixture. Arrange stuffed shells in a single layer over the sauce. Cover shells with remaining 3 cups sauce; pour water evenly over sauce. (Don't be concerned about the watery appearance; the shells will absorb it during the cooking process.) Cover dish with foil and bake for 50 minutes. Remove foil and bake another 10 minutes.

Hint: This quick dish freezes well and can be warmed in the microwave.

When buying canned tomatoes, look for products that have no added salt. Growers allow these tomatoes to ripen on the vines longer, to preserve more natural flavor.

Nutrition Analysis Per Serving:

Calories 285

Protein 19g

Carbohydrate 39g

Fat 5g

(Saturated 2g)

Cholesterol 13mg

Fiber 3g

Sodium 956mg

Rigatoni Casserole

Yield:
4 servings

Serving Size:
1 ½ cups

Preparation Time:
20–25 minutes

Cooking Time:
20 minutes

Nutrition Analysis Per Serving:

Calories 366

Protein 24g

Carbohydrate 44g

Fat 10g

(*Saturated 4g*)

Cholesterol 22mg

Fiber 4g

Sodium 808mg

1 ¾ c. rigatoni, uncooked
1 lb. firm tofu, mashed
¼ c. grated Parmesan cheese
1 tsp. Italian seasoning
½ tsp. garlic powder
½ tsp. onion powder
1 jar (25-oz.) chunky vegetable pasta sauce
1 c. shredded mozzarella cheese
Cooking spray

Cook the pasta according to package directions until *al dente*. Drain and rinse. Combine the tofu, Parmesan cheese, Italian spice blend, garlic powder, and onion powder in a bowl and mix well. Layer the pasta sauce, pasta, tofu mixture, and mozzarella cheese ½ at a time in a 2-quart baking dish coated with cooking spray. Bake at 350° for 20 minutes.

Creamy Lentils over Pasta

½ c. brown lentils
8 oz. pasta
1 small onion, finely chopped
3 cloves garlic, minced
1 T. canola oil
1 tsp. cumin
1 tsp. ground ginger
½ tsp. red pepper flakes
1 can (16 oz.) diced tomatoes, undrained
1 ¼ c. vegetable broth or water
1 T. sugar
½ c. plain nonfat or lowfat yogurt
2 T. finely shredded fresh basil

Yield:
4 servings

Serving Size:
1 cup

Preparation Time:
15 minutes

Cooking Time:
35 minutes

Rinse and sort small rocks and debris from the lentils. Sauté the onion and garlic in the canola oil in a saucepan for 5 minutes or until the onion is tender. Stir in cumin, ginger, and red pepper flakes. Sauté for 1 minute longer. Add lentils, undrained tomatoes, broth, and sugar; mix well. Simmer for 20–25 minutes or until lentils are tender, stirring occasionally. Meanwhile, cook pasta. Cover to keep warm. Remove lentils from heat. Stir in the yogurt and basil. Arrange pasta on a serving platter. Spoon the lentils over pasta; serve warm.

Try displacing the fatty foods in your diet by choosing complex carbohydrates: Starchy vegetables, fresh fruit, legumes, grains, pastas, breads, and whole-grain cereals are examples of complex carbs that can be flavorful, filling alternatives to high-fat foods. They are also loaded with fiber.

Nutrition Analysis Per Serving:

Calories 389

Protein 22g

Carbohydrate 65g

Fat 5g

(Saturated <1g)

Cholesterol 1mg

Fiber 10g

Sodium 531mg

Long-Life Noodles

A fabulous meal for an office party or family gathering.

Yield:
8 servings

Serving Size:
2 cups

Preparation Time:
25–30 minutes

Cooking Time:
5 minutes

Nutrition Analysis Per Serving:

Calories 386

Protein 15g

Carbohydrate 61g

Fat 9g

(Saturated 2g)

Cholesterol 80mg

Fiber 6g

Sodium 202mg

Peanut Sauce:
¼ c. smooth peanut butter
¼ c. hot water
3 cloves garlic, minced
3 green onions, chopped
2 T. low-sodium soy sauce
2 T. red wine vinegar
1 T. canola oil
1 T. sugar
½ tsp. cayenne pepper

Toppings and Pasta:
5 oz. snow peas
Cooking spray
3 eggs, beaten
2 c. fresh julienne-cut spinach
2 large carrots, shredded
4 green onions, diagonally sliced
18 oz. fresh pasta, cooked and chilled

For sauce, combine all ingredients in a blender or food processor until smooth. For toppings, steam the snow peas in a steamer until tender; drain and slice into strips. Coat a small non-stick skillet with cooking spray. Pour eggs into skillet, tilting to cover bottom to form a thin pancake. Cook over medium heat until firm, turning once. Invert onto a plate. Cut the egg into thin strips.

Arrange snow peas, egg, spinach, carrots, and green onions on a platter. Spoon pasta on to plates. Have guests add toppings and sauce.

Desserts

Chocolaty Fruit Burritos

Yield:
4 servings

Serving Size:
1 burrito

Preparation Time:
5–7 minutes

2 c. fresh strawberries, cleaned, and sliced
8 oz. vanilla-flavored nonfat or lowfat yogurt
4 (6-inch) flour tortillas or prepared crêpes
⅓ c. chocolate syrup
Fresh berries for garnish

In a small bowl, combine berries with yogurt; mix well. Place ¼ of the mixture on each tortilla and roll up. Place each burrito, seam side down, on a small plate and spoon chocolate syrup evenly over each burrito. Garnish with a few fresh berries.

Nutrition Analysis Per Serving:

Calories 234

Protein 7g

Carbohydrate 45g

Fat 4g

(Saturated <1g)

Cholesterol 1mg

Fiber 2g

Sodium 276mg

Redstone Rhubarb Crisp

6 c. fresh or frozen rhubarb, diced
Cooking spray
½ c. packed brown sugar
⅓ c. flour
⅓ c. regular oats, uncooked
½ tsp. cinnamon
2 T. margarine

Preheat oven to 350°. Place rhubarb in an
8-inch-square baking pan lightly coated
with cooking spray. In a small bowl combine
brown sugar, flour, oats, and cinnamon. Cut
in margarine until consistency of coarse meal.
Sprinkle mixture over rhubarb; then bake for
30 minutes or until topping is lightly browned.

Yield:
6 servings

Serving Size:
½ cup

Preparation Time:
15 minutes

Cooking Time:
30 minutes

**Nutrition Analysis
Per Serving:**

Calories 171

Protein 2g

Carbohydrate 32g

Fat 4g

(Saturated 1g)

Cholesterol 0mg

Fiber 3g

Sodium 57mg

Bananas Grand Marnier

This special dessert is irresistible!

Yield:
4 servings

Serving Size:
½ cup

Preparation Time:
5 minutes

Cooking Time:
3–5 minutes

1 T. margarine
⅓ c. orange juice
½ T. honey
2 T. Grand Marnier or other
orange-flavored liqueur
¼ tsp. vanilla
3 bananas, sliced
Ground cinnamon

Melt margarine in a saucepan; stir in orange juice, honey, Grand Marnier, and vanilla. Add bananas and simmer about 3 minutes or until thoroughly heated, stirring frequently. Serve warm, garnished with cinnamon.

Note: Also good served over vanilla lowfat frozen yogurt.

Nutrition Analysis Per Serving:

Calories 149

Protein 1g

Carbohydrate 28g

Fat 3g

(Saturated 1g)

Cholesterol 0mg

Fiber 2g

Sodium 35mg

Bananas that are beginning to turn brown should be stored in the refrigerator to slow down ripening. The skin will turn black but the fruit will not be over-ripe.

Caramel Bananas

4 large ripe bananas
Cooking spray
⅓ c. packed brown sugar
1 T. margarine, melted
1 ½ tsp. lemon juice
¼ tsp. cinnamon
1 ½ c. nonfat or lowfat vanilla frozen yogurt

Cut the bananas lengthwise into halves. Arrange the banana halves cut sides up on a baking sheet coated with cooking spray. Bake at 450° for 4 minutes. Combine the brown sugar, margarine, lemon juice, and cinnamon in a bowl and mix well. Drizzle over the bananas. Bake for 3 minutes longer. Cut each banana half crosswise into 3 equal portions. Arrange over the yogurt in dessert bowls. Top with any extra sauce.

Yield:
4 servings

Serving Size:
6 banana pieces with ¼ of sauce

Preparation Time:
5 minutes

Cooking Time:
7 minutes

Nutrition Analysis Per Serving:

Calories 358

Protein 8g

Carbohydrate 72g

Fat 7g

(Saturated 2g)

Cholesterol 38mg

Fiber 4g

Sodium 79mg

Western Slope Peach Melba

Yield:
4 servings

Serving Size:
1 cup

Preparation Time:
5 minutes

Cooking Time:
3 minutes

1 pkg. (12 oz.) frozen raspberries
2 T. raspberry jelly or spread
2 peaches, sliced
2 c. nonfat or lowfat vanilla frozen yogurt

Combine raspberries and jelly in a glass bowl.
Microwave on medium for 2–3 minutes or
until raspberries are slightly warm; stir to mix
in jelly. Divide peaches evenly into 4 bowls; top
with ½ cup scoop of yogurt. Pour raspberry
sauce evenly over 4 portions and serve.

**Nutrition Analysis
Per Serving:**

Calories 163

Protein 6g

Carbohydrate 45g

Fat <1g

(Saturated <1g)

Cholesterol 0mg

Fiber 2g

Sodium 65mg

Chocolate Meringue Kisses

Served with fresh fruit, these light, sweet cookies are almost guilt free (only 12 calories apiece!).

3 egg whites, at room temperature
¼ tsp. cream of tartar
½ c. sugar
3 T. cocoa powder
1 tsp. vanilla

Preheat oven to 200°. Line two baking sheets with aluminum foil; set aside. In a small bowl, beat egg whites and cream of tartar at high speed of an electric mixer until soft peaks form. Gradually add sugar 2 tablespoons at a time, beating after each addition until sugar is dissolved. Add cocoa powder and vanilla; continue beating until stiff, glossy peaks form. Spoon meringue by the tablespoonful onto baking sheets forming chocolate kiss shapes. Bake 50–60 minutes or until set. Let cool on cookie sheets for 10 minutes. Carefully loosen and remove cookies with spatula and completely cool them on wire racks. Store in an airtight container.

Cocoa is much lower in fat than baking chocolate, and it doesn't have the high saturated fat content.

Yield:
40 servings

Serving Size:
1 cookie

Preparation Time:
20 minutes

Cooking Time:
50–60 minutes

Nutrition Analysis Per Serving:

Calories 12

Protein <1g

Carbohydrate 3g

Fat <1g

(Saturated <1g)

Cholesterol 0mg

Fiber <1g

Sodium 4mg

Cappuccino Cheesecake

Yield:
12 servings

Serving Size:
$^1/_{12}$ of cheesecake

Preparation Time:
20–25 minutes

Cooking Time:
65–70 minutes

Chilling Time:
4–10 hours

**Nutrition Analysis
Per Serving:**

Calories 219

Protein 10g

Carbohydrate 27g

Fat 7g

(Saturated 5g)

Cholesterol 21mg

Fiber <1g

Sodium 363mg

½ c. chocolate wafer crumbs
Cooking spray
3 T. instant espresso powder
3 T. coffee liqueur
1 ½ c. 1% cottage cheese
1 block (8 oz.) light cream cheese, softened
1 tub (8 oz.) light cream cheese
1 c. sugar
2 T. flour
6 egg whites
¼ tsp. cinnamon
¼ tsp. salt

Preheat oven to 325°. Reserve 1 teaspoon of the crumbs. Sprinkle the remaining crumbs over the bottom or a 9-inch spring-form pan coated with cooking spray. Combine the espresso powder and liqueur in a bowl, stirring until the powder dissolves. Process the cottage cheese in a blender until smooth. Add the cream cheese, sugar, flour, egg whites, cinnamon, salt, and espresso mixture. Process until blended. Spoon into the prepared pan. Bake for 65 to 70 minutes or until cheesecake puffs and the center is almost set. Sprinkle with the reserved crumbs. Cool in pan on a wire rack. Chill, covered, for 4–10 hours. Remove side of pan and slice.

Light Tiramisu

While our recipe is certainly not low in fat and calories, it beats the 35 grams of fat and 440 calories found in traditional versions.

8 oz. mascarpone cheese, softened
4 oz. light cream cheese, softened
½ c. confectioners' sugar
1 c. frozen light whipped topping, thawed
⅔ c. hot water
2 tsp. instant coffee granules
¼ c. brandy or coffee liqueur
2 pkgs. (3 oz. each) ladyfingers
1 ½ tsp. baking cocoa

Combine the mascarpone cheese, cream cheese, and confectioners' sugar in a bowl. Beat until smooth, scraping the bowl occasionally. Fold in the whipped topping. Bring hot water to a boil in a saucepan. Add the coffee granules, stirring until the granules dissolve. Let stand until cool. Stir in the brandy.

Arrange 1 package of the ladyfingers over the bottom and up the side of a 2-quart soufflé dish. Drizzle or brush with half the coffee mixture. Spread with half the mascarpone cheese mixture. Repeat the layering process with the remaining ladyfingers, remaining coffee mixture, and remaining mascarpone cheese mixture Sift the baking cocoa over the top. Chill, covered, for 8–10 hours.

Yield:
10 servings

Serving Size:
1 cup

Preparation Time:
20–25 minutes

Chilling Time:
8–10 hours

Nutrition Analysis Per Serving:

Calories 246

Protein 5g

Carbohydrate 20g

Fat 15g

(Saturated 8g)

Cholesterol 98mg

Fiber <1g

Sodium 72mg

Fresh Strawberry Torte

A very light and elegant ending to any summertime gathering.

Yield:
8 servings

Serving Size:
⅛ torte

Preparation Time:
20 minutes

Cooking Time:
30 minutes

Chilling Time:
2–10 hours

Nutrition Analysis Per Serving:

Calories 243

Protein 3g

Carbohydrate 35g

Fat 9g

(Saturated 4g)

Cholesterol 0mg

Fiber 2g

Sodium 106mg

3 egg whites
¾ c. sugar
1 tsp. vanilla extract
¾ c. finely crushed soda crackers
½ c. chopped pecans
Cooking spray
1 lb. strawberries, hulled and sliced
1 T. Grand Marnier or other orange liqueur
8 oz. frozen light whipped topping, thawed

Preheat oven to 325°. Beat the egg whites in a mixer bowl until soft peaks form. Add the sugar gradually, beating constantly. Add the vanilla. Beat until stiff peaks form. Fold in the cracker crumbs and pecans. Spread over the bottom and up the side of a 9-inch pie plate coated with non-stick cooking spray. Bake at 325° for 30 minutes or until light brown. Let stand until cool. Mound the strawberries in the meringue crust. Drizzle with the Grand Marnier and spread with the whipped topping. Chill, covered, for 2–10 hours. Garnish with additional strawberries.

Tip: This recipe can easily be doubled for large crowds. Spread the meringue in a circle on a greased baking sheet instead of spreading in a pie plate if desired.

Small amounts of liqueurs or wine can be used sparingly to add sophistication, moisture, and flavor to desserts.

Easy Spiced Apple

1 medium apple
⅛ tsp. cinnamon
1 T. raisins
1 T. chopped nuts
⅓ c. nonfat or lowfat vanilla
frozen yogurt (optional)

Core apple and cut into bite-size chunks;
place in a small dish. Sprinkle with cinnamon;
cover and microwave on high for 1–2 minutes.
Sprinkle with raisins and nuts and serve.
Dollop with frozen yogurt if desired.

Yield:
1 serving

Serving Size:
1 apple

Preparation Time:
3 minutes

Cooking Time:
2 minutes

**Nutrition Analysis
Per Serving:**

Calories 151

Protein 1g

Carbohydrate 27g

Fat 6g

(Saturated 1g)

Cholesterol 0mg

Fiber 5g

Sodium 2mg

Pears Poached in Wine Sauce

This elegant dessert makes a wonderful dish to serve when company comes.

Yield:
4 servings

Serving Size:
1 pear

Preparation Time:
15–20 minutes

Cooking Time:
20 minutes

1 ½ c. dry red wine
1 c. water
½ c. packed dark brown sugar
3 T. honey
1 T. fresh lemon juice
1 tsp. vanilla extract
1 (3-inch) cinnamon stick, broken in half
10 black peppercorns
8 whole cloves
4 firm ripe Bartlett or Bosc pears
2 T. cornstarch

Nutrition Analysis Per Serving:

Calories 330

Protein 1g

Carbohydrate 70g

Fat 1g

(Saturated <1g)

Cholesterol 0mg

Fiber 4g

Sodium 16mg

Combine all ingredients except cornstarch, in a 3-quart microwave-safe dish; mix well. Microwave on high for 5 minutes until mixture comes to a boil. Peel and core pears, leaving stems intact (see the tip, below). Arrange pears stem up in mixture. Microwave, covered, for 10 minutes or until pears are tender. Cool 5 minutes. Remove pears to a platter. Strain poaching liquid, discarding the spices. Pour half the liquid into a microwave-safe dish, discarding the rest. Mix cornstarch with enough water in a bowl to form a thin paste. Whisk cornstarch mixture into poaching liquid. Microwave on medium for 5 minutes or until sauce thickens. Spoon part of sauce into 4 dessert bowls. Arrange 1 pear in each bowl. Drizzle remaining sauce over pears.

Tip: To core a pear, hold fruit in one hand. Using a small paring knife cut a hole about ½–inch in diameter through bottom of pear, stopping ¾ of the way up. Discard core. Cut ¼-inch off base of pear.

Fruit Custard Dessert Pizza

Crust:
½ c. lowfat small curd cottage cheese
3 T. margarine, softened
1 T. plain nonfat or lowfat yogurt
1 c. flour
½ c. regular oats, uncooked
1 tsp. grated lemon peel
¼ tsp. salt
Cooking spray

Topping:
½ c. low-sugar orange marmalade
1 pkg. (1.9 oz.) instant vanilla pudding
2 c. skim milk
1 orange, peeled and sliced in half moons
3 kiwis, peeled and sliced
1 pint strawberries, stemmed and cut in half
1 banana, peeled and sliced
¼ fresh pineapple, peeled and in chunks

In small bowl, combine cottage cheese, margarine and yogurt. Beat until smooth. In a bowl combine flour, oats, lemon peel, and salt. Stir cheese mixture into flour mixture; form into ball. Press evenly into a 12-inch pizza pan coated with cooking spray. Form a rim ½-inch above the edge and crimp. Bake crust at 400° for 15–20 minutes and cool.

Topping: Heat marmalade until melted; set aside. Prepare pudding according to package directions using 2 cups skim milk. Spread pudding into cooled crust. Arrange fruit atop pudding and drizzle with marmalade. Cover and chill for 2 hours.

Yield:
8 servings

Serving Size:
1 wedge

Preparation Time:
25 minutes

Cooking Time:
15–20 minutes

Chilling Time:
2 hours

Nutrition Analysis Per Serving:

Calories 255

Protein 7g

Carbohydrate 46g

Fat 5g

(Saturated 1g)

Cholesterol 2mg

Fiber 4g

Sodium 309mg

Cherries in the Snow

Yield:
10 servings

Serving Size:
1/10 of pie

Preparation Time:
25 minutes (plus 1
day ahead)

Cooking Time:
8–10 minutes

Chilling Time:
4 hours

**Nutrition Analysis
Per Serving:**

Calories 360

Protein 7g

Carbohydrate 63g

Fat 9g

(Saturated 4g)

Cholesterol 17mg

Fiber 1g

Sodium 268mg

1 large container (32 oz.) vanilla-
flavored lowfat yogurt
1 c. graham cracker crumbs
3 T. margarine, melted
¼ c. sugar
1 envelope unflavored gelatin
⅓ c. lemon juice
¾ c. sugar
1 tub (8 oz.) light cream cheese
2 tsp. grated lemon peel
1 can (21 oz.) cherry pie filling

Place colander in a large bowl; line colander
with 2 coffee filters. Make yogurt cheese by
spooning yogurt into colander, covering loosely
with plastic wrap, and chilling for 24 hours.
Discard liquid. Preheat oven to 350°. Combine
graham cracker crumbs, margarine, and sugar;
mix well and press into a 9-inch pie plate. Bake
for 8–10 minutes. Cool completely. In a small
saucepan, sprinkle gelatin over lemon juice;
let stand 1 minute. Add remaining sugar and
cook over low heat, stirring until gelatin and
sugar dissolve. Remove from heat; place in a
blender. Add cream cheese, lemon peel, and
chilled yogurt cheese; blend until smooth.
Pour into crust; cover and chill for 4 hours.
Spoon cherry pie filling over top and serve.

*Yogurt cheese is great on bagels or bread. It will
keep in the refrigerator for up to one week.*

Fresh Fruit Parfait

Fruit becomes elegant in a parfait glass with this easy recipe.

1 c. plain nonfat or lowfat yogurt
2 T. maple syrup
1 tsp. vanilla
½ tsp. cinnamon
2 medium bananas, sliced
2 c. strawberries, sliced

Combine yogurt, syrup, vanilla, and cinnamon. Layer bananas and strawberries in parfait glasses with sauce between each layer.

Yield:
4 servings

Serving Size:
1 parfait

Preparation Time:
10–15 minutes

Nutrition Analysis Per Serving:

Calories 132

Protein 4g

Carbohydrate 31g

Fat <1g

(Saturated <1g)

Cholesterol 1mg

Fiber 3g

Sodium 36mg

Frozen Pumpkin Squares

Yield:
18 servings

Serving Size:
3 x 2-inch piece

Preparation Time:
10–15 minutes

Freezing Time:
4–6 hours

2 c. cooked or canned pumpkin
½ c. sugar
1 tsp. ground ginger
½ tsp. nutmeg
½ gal. nonfat or lowfat vanilla frozen yogurt
4 dozen gingersnaps

Combine pumpkin, sugar, and spices; stir in yogurt. Line bottom of a 13 x 9 x 2-inch pan with half of the gingersnaps. Pour half of pumpkin mixture over gingersnaps. Repeat layers and freeze. To serve, let sit at room temperature for 5 minutes; cut into squares.

**Nutrition Analysis
Per Serving:**

Calories 171

Protein 5g

Carbohydrate 40g

Fat 3g

(*Saturated 1g*)

Cholesterol 0mg

Fiber 1g

Sodium 122mg

Boulder Canyon Carrot Cake

This cake is moist and tasty, with or without frosting.

Cooking spray
1 c. boiling water
2 c. finely shredded carrots
1 c. crushed pineapple with juice
⅔ c. shredded wheat-bran cereal
1 ¼ c. sugar
1 c. whole-wheat flour
1 c. flour
3 eggs
½ c. raisins
½ c. chopped walnuts
¼ c. oil
1 ¼ tsp. baking soda
1 tsp. vanilla
1 tsp. each cinnamon, nutmeg,
ground cloves, and salt

Yield:
18 servings

Serving Size:
3 x 2 ½-inch piece

Preparation Time:
30 minutes

Cooking Time:
40–45 minutes

Preheat oven to 350°. Coat a 13 x 9 x 2-inch pan with cooking spray and dust with flour; set aside. Pour boiling water over carrots; set aside. In a large mixing bowl, combine crushed pineapple and cereal; let stand 5 minutes. Beat carrots and all remaining ingredients into cereal mixture at low speed on an electric mixer for 1 minute, scraping bowl constantly. Increase to medium speed; mix for 2 minutes. Pour batter into prepared pan. Bake for 40–45 minutes or until wooden pick inserted in center comes out clean. Serve with a sprinkle of powdered sugar.

Nutrition Analysis Per Serving:

Calories 196

Protein 4g

Carbohydrate 33g

Fat 7g

(Saturated 1g)

Cholesterol 35mg

Fiber 3g

Sodium 245mg

Strawberry-Lemon Trifle

*For the Fourth of July, make this with blueberries and strawberries
—a truly patriotic dessert.*

Yield:
16 servings

Serving Size:
1 cup

Preparation Time:
15–20 minutes

1 pkg. (3 ½ oz.) instant vanilla pudding
1 ¾ c. skim milk
12 oz. lowfat lemon flavored yogurt
1 angel food cake
1 qt. fresh strawberries, hulled and diced
⅓ c. sliced almonds, toasted

Prepare vanilla pudding according to package directions using 1 ¾ cup skim milk. After pudding has thickened, add yogurt and stir until blended. Cut angel food cake into 1-inch cubes. To assemble trifle, place ⅓ of cake cubes on bottom or a deep glass bowl; spread ⅓ of pudding mixture over cubes; then top with ⅓ of sliced berries. Repeat layers of cake, pudding, and strawberries 2 more times. Top with toasted sliced almonds.

Hint: Use other fruit in season such as peaches, raspberries, and kiwi.

Nutrition Analysis Per Serving:

Calories 169

Protein 5g

Carbohydrate 36g

Fat 1g

(Saturated <1g)

Cholesterol 2mg

Fiber 1g

Sodium 248mg

To toast nuts, cover bottom of microwave with wax paper. Spread with ¼ cup chopped nuts. Microwave uncovered on high for 5 minutes or until lightly browned. Nuts can also be toasted in a skillet on the stove or in a toaster oven. Be careful to watch them to prevent burning.

Glazed Cranberry Cake

Looking for that extra-special dessert? You've found it! For a twist make this with raspberries instead of cranberries.

2 c. flour
⅔ c. sugar
2 tsp. baking powder
⅔ c. skim milk
1 egg, beaten
3 T. canola oil
½ tsp. lemon extract
2 c. whole cranberries, washed,
Cooking Spray

Lemon Sauce:
⅓ c. sugar
1 T. cornstarch
1 c. boiling water
3 T. lemon juice
2 T. margarine
1 T. grated lemon peel

Yield:
12 servings

Serving Size:
¹/₁₂ of 9-inch cake
2 tablespoons of
sauce

Preparation Time:
10–15 minutes

Cooking Time:
40 minutes

Preheat oven to 350°. Combine flour, sugar, and baking powder in a bowl. In another bowl, stir milk, egg, oil, and lemon extract. Pour milk mixture into flour mixture and blend well. Stir in cranberries. Pour into a sprayed 9-inch-round cake pan. Bake for 40 minutes. Serve warm, topped with lemon sauce.

For sauce: combine sugar and cornstarch in a saucepan. Gradually add boiling water, stirring constantly with a whisk. Cook over medium until thick and clear. Add lemon juice, margarine, and lemon peel. Stir until margarine melts. Serve warm.

Nutrition Analysis Per Serving:

Calories 213

Protein 3g

Carbohydrate 37g

Fat 6g

(Saturated 1g)

Cholesterol 18mg

Fiber 1g

Sodium 117mg

Fresh Apple Cake

For those of you with an ample supply of apples, this is a delightfully delicious dessert!

Yield:
18 servings

Serving Size:
3 x 2 ½-inch piece

Preparation Time:
20 minutes

Cooking Time:
40 minutes

2 eggs, beaten
1 ¼ c. sugar
⅓ c. canola oil
4 c. grated apples (about 4–6 apples)
2 c. flour
2 tsp. cinnamon
1 tsp. baking soda
½ c. chopped nuts
Cooking spray
2 T. powdered sugar

Preheat oven to 350°. Stir eggs, sugar, and oil together with a spoon. Stir in grated apple, flour, cinnamon, and baking soda; mix well. Add chopped nuts. Pour into a 13 x 9 x 2-inch baking pan lightly coated with cooking spray. Bake for 40 minutes. Let cool, then sprinkle with powdered sugar.

Nutrition Analysis Per Serving:

Calories 196

Protein 3g

Carbohydrate 31g

Fat 7g

(Saturated 1g)

Cholesterol 24mg

Fiber 2g

Sodium 78mg

Orange Pound Cake

This is an unbelievably light cake, and it comes with a delightful chocolate variation.

Cooking spray
1 ½ c. flour
¾ c. sugar
2 tsp. baking powder
½ c. canola oil
½ c. orange juice
1 tsp. grated orange peel
4 egg whites, stiffly beaten

Preheat oven to 350°. Coat the bottom of a 5 x 9-inch loaf pan with cooking spray; dust with flour and set aside. Combine flour, sugar, and baking powder in a large bowl; add oil and orange juice. Beat until well blended (batter will be thick). Add orange peel and about ⅓ of egg whites; stir gently. Fold in remaining egg whites. Spoon batter into prepared pan. Bake for 45 minutes or until done. Cool in pan for 10 minutes, then remove from pan and cool on wire rack. Cut into 16 even slices.

Variation: For *Chocolate Pound Cake,* eliminate orange juice and orange peel; add ⅓ cup cocoa to flour mixture. Add ½ cup nonfat milk, 1 tablespoon vanilla, and 1 teaspoon chocolate flavoring to oil.

Reprinted with permission from HealthMark Centers, Inc.

Yield:
1 loaf

Serving Size:
1 slice

Preparation Time:
15 minutes

Cooking Time:
45 minutes

Nutrition Analysis Per Serving:

Calories 149

Protein 2g

Carbohydrate 19g

Fat 7g

(*Saturated 1g*)

Cholesterol 0mg

Fiber <1g

Sodium 83mg

Chocolate Surprise Bundt Cake

For the chocoholic—a chocolate cake with a surprise in each bite.

Yield:
16 servings

Serving Size:
1 wedge

Preparation Time:
15–20 minutes

Cooking Time:
40–50 minutes

Cooking spray
½ c. dried apricots, chopped
½ c. chocolate chips
½ c. chopped walnuts
1 T. cornstarch
1 box chocolate cake mix
2 eggs
1 ½ c. lowfat buttermilk
Powdered sugar

Preheat oven to 350°. Coat a 12-cup Bundt pan with cooking spray; dust with flour and set aside. Combine apricots, chocolate chips, walnuts, and cornstarch in a small bowl; stir to coat and set aside. Combine cake mix, eggs, and buttermilk in a large mixing bowl; mix at low speed with an electric mixer until blended. Fold in apricot and nut mixture. Pour into prepared Bundt pan and bake 40–50 minutes. Cool in pan for 25 minutes; then turn out on a cooling rack. Sprinkle top with powdered sugar before serving.

**Nutrition Analysis
Per Serving:**

Calories 219

Protein 5g

Carbohydrate 31g

Fat 9g

(Saturated 3g)

Cholesterol 35mg

Fiber 2g

Sodium 286mg

Buttermilk actually contains no butter and usually has very little fat. Most buttermilk today is made from skim or lowfat milk.

Bread Pudding with Rum Sauce

6 slices whole-wheat or white bread
2 c. skim milk
1 T. margarine
4 egg whites, beaten
⅔ c. sugar
½ c. raisins
½ tsp. cinnamon
¼ tsp. nutmeg
1 tsp. vanilla

Rum Sauce:
1 c. skim milk
2 T. brown sugar
4 tsp. cornstarch
4 tsp. dark rum

Yield:
6 servings

Serving Size:
4 x 2 ½-inch piece
3 tablespoons sauce

Preparation Time:
10 minutes

Cooking Time:
15 minutes

Cut bread slices into cubes. Place bread in an 8 x 8 x 2-inch microwave-safe baking dish; set aside. Combine milk and margarine in a glass bowl; microwave on high for 3 minutes. Mix a small amount of hot milk into beaten egg whites. Pour remaining egg mixture into milk. Add sugar, raisins, cinnamon, nutmeg, and vanilla; stir. Pour mixture over bread cubes. Microwave uncovered on high for 7 minutes. Continue to cooking unil center is firm.

For sauce, combine milk, sugar, cornstarch, and rum in a glass bowl; stir well. Microwave, uncovered, on high for 2–3 minutes, stirring occasionally. Serve over warm bread pudding.

Nutrition Analysis Per Serving:

Calories 297

Protein 10g

Carbohydrate 57g

Fat 3g

(Saturated 1g)

Cholesterol 2mg

Fiber 3g

Sodium 273mg

Granny Smith Apple Crisp

This light and crispy dessert has a sweet-tart flavor that only Granny Smith apples can provide.

Yield:
6 servings

Serving Size:
⅔ cup

Preparation Time:
20 minutes

Cooking Time:
25–30 minutes

⅓ c. regular oats, uncooked
2 T. brown sugar
1 T. flour
1 T. margarine, melted
4 T. unsweetened apple juice concentrate, thawed and divided
3–4 Granny Smith apples (1 ½ lbs.), cored and cut into ½-inch slices
½ tsp. cinnamon
¼ tsp. nutmeg
½ tsp. grated lemon peel (optional)

Preheat oven to 400°. Mix oats, sugar, flour, margarine, and 1 tablespoon apple juice concentrate into a small bowl; set mixture aside for topping. Place apples in large bowl. Add cinnamon, nutmeg, lemon peel, and remaining 3 tablespoons apple juice concentrate; toss well. Mound apples in an 8-inch pie plate or 2-quart casserole dish; sprinkle with topping mixture. Bake 25–30 minutes or until brown.

Nutrition Analysis Per Serving:

Calories 126

Protein 1g

Carbohydrate 28g

Fat 2g

(Saturated <1g)

Cholesterol 0mg

Fiber 3g

Sodium 28mg

Nutty Apricot Delights

½ c. chopped dried apricots
½ c. chopped nuts
⅓ c. flaked coconut
⅓ c. sugar
⅓ c. chopped dates
1 egg
2 T. sugar

In a glass bowl combine all ingredients except 2 tablespoons of sugar. Microwave, uncovered, on high for 5–6 minutes or until mixture thickens enough to hold its shape. Cool completely. Form into 1-inch balls; then roll in remaining sugar.

Coconut is cholesterol free, but like the oil that comes from it, coconut is high in saturated fat. For that reason, use it sparingly.

Yield:
24 sevings

Serving Size:
1 cookie

Preparation Time:
15 minutes

Cooking Time:
5–6 minutes

Nutrition Analysis Per Serving:

Calories 53

Protein 1g

Carbohydrate 8g

Fat 2g

(Saturated 1g)

Cholesterol 9mg

Fiber 1g

Sodium 6mg

Banana-Oatmeal Cookies

Whether you're trail blazing, half-piping, or simply hanging out, you'll want a few of these on hand to tame the mountain munchies.

Yield:
48 servings

Serving Size:
1 cookie

Preparation Time:
15 minutes

Cooking Time:
10–12 minutes

1 ½ c. flour
1 c. sugar
¾ tsp. cinnamon
½ tsp. baking soda
½ tsp. salt
¼ tsp. nutmeg
¾ c. margarine
1 ¾ c. quick-cooking oats, uncooked
1 c. (2–3) mashed ripe bananas
1 egg, beaten
⅓ c. nuts, chopped
Cooking spray

Preheat oven to 400°. Combine flour and next 5 ingredients. Cut in margarine with a pastry blender or fork until mixture resembles coarse meal. Add oats, mashed bananas, egg, and nuts; mix thoroughly. Drop by teaspoonfuls onto a cookie sheet that's been lightly coated with cooking spray. Bake 10–12 minutes.

Nutrition Analysis Per Serving:

Calories 82

Protein 1g

Carbohydrate 11g

Fat 4g

(Saturated 1g)

Cholesterol 4mg

Fiber 1g

Sodium 72mg

Which would you choose: An oatmeal cookie or a granola bar? Some brand-name oatmeal cookies have half the calories and as much as 60% less fat than some granola bars.

Index

Notes